ALL
THE
LIGHTS
ON

ALL THE LIGHTS ON

REIMAGINING THEATER WITH TEN THOUSAND THINGS

MICHELLE HENSLEY  MINNESOTA HISTORICAL SOCIETY PRESS

PUBLISHED IN ASSOCIATION WITH HOWLROUND: A CENTER FOR THE THEATER COMMONS

The publication of this book was supported through a generous grant from the Atherton and Winifred (Wollaeger) Bean Fund for Business History

www.mnhspress.org

The Minnesota Historical Society Press is a member of the Association of American University Presses.

Manufactured in the United States of America

10 9 8 7 6 5 4 3 2 1

♾ The paper used in this publication meets the minimum requirements of the American National Standard for Information Sciences—Permanence for Printed Library Materials, ANSI Z39.48–1984.

International Standard Book Number

ISBN: 978-0-87351-983-0 (paper)
ISBN: 978-0-87351-984-7 (e-book)

Library of Congress Cataloging-in-Publication Data

Hensley, Michelle. All the lights on : reimagining theater with Ten Thousand Things / Michelle Hensley.
    pages cm
Summary: "A history of the Twin Cities' theater company Ten Thousand Things, which for more than twenty years has been bringing intelligent, lively theater to nontraditional audiences as well as the general public"—Provided by publisher.
ISBN 978-0-87351-983-0 (paperback)—ISBN 978-0-87351-984-7 (ebook)
1. Ten Thousand Things (Theater company)—History. I. Title.
PN2297.T46H46 2015
792.09776'579—dc23
                                                                                2014043270

This and other Minnesota Historical Society Press books are available from popular e-book vendors.

Cover: Sally Wingert and Isabell Monk O'Connor in *Twelfth Night*, Dorothy Day Center, St. Paul. Insets: Barbara Kingsley in *The Good Person of Szechwan*, women's correctional facility; audience at men's correctional facility; Peter Vitale plays music for *Twelfth Night*, Dorothy Day Center. All photos by Paula Keller.

Interior: Photos pages 20, 120, 156, 194 by Tom Wallace. Photos pages 40, 98, 154, 196 by Keri Pickett. All other photos by Paula Keller.

To the audiences and artists of **TEN THOUSAND THINGS**

CONTENTS

ALL
THE
LIGHTS
ON

INTRODUCTION

A LITTLE BAG OF SILVER

MY FAVORITE PLAY IS *The Good Person of Szech-wan* by Bertolt Brecht. In it, a poor woman named Shen Te gets a gift—a bag of silver from the gods. She has to figure out how to spend it wisely. It's all she has.

When I was in my early twenties, I knew I loved theater and thought it might be what I wanted to spend my life on. But I also knew I had only one life. I wanted to be sure I could use it to give something back to the world. I wrestled with this almost every day throughout my twenties, through college and grad school and in between. With so many overwhelming problems on the planet—most humans living in desperate poverty, struggling each day with violence and hunger, pollution threatening our very existence—I didn't see how theater could help very much.

Also, I honestly couldn't imagine myself going down the recommended path for aspiring young directors, climbing the ladder at a regional theater. I sensed I would need to act a "part" and squeeze myself into some kind of mold of authority and confidence in order to prove that I had "the stuff" to be a director. If I worked hard to ingratiate myself with those in charge, I might eventually be allowed to direct a reading of a script I probably wouldn't even like, then after more time, perhaps a staged reading of another script I didn't really care about—all for very little if any pay. I knew that if I couldn't find the space to truly be myself and work on things I loved, my art wouldn't be very good.

Most important, some things about theater itself made me uncomfortable. Looking around at the audience before the lights went down, I saw mostly well-off, educated white people. Lots of other people seemed left out. I thought of my grandfather, an Iowa farmer who lost his land in the Depression. He usual-

1

ly wore striped engineer overalls and a seed corn cap. He was very intelligent but never went to college. I imagined he would feel out of place walking into most of the theaters I'd been to, both the scruffy little black boxes and the big theaters with their fancy lobbies. And he probably wouldn't be interested in much of what was happening up on the stage, certainly not most nonlinear experimental theater and performance art (much of which I personally enjoyed) but also not even many of the classic plays done on big regional stages, where the audience had to sit so far away. I imagined much of it would feel pretentious to him, or at least very puzzling, and certainly remote. I really didn't want to spend my life on an art form that seemed set up to leave so many people out.

I grew up in the very white, very middle-class world of Des Moines, Iowa, in the sixties and early seventies, in a period of American history that now is starting to look like an aberrant bubble of relative income equality. The wealth then was distributed in such a way that taxes supported a very good public school system and other social safety nets, and employers generally shared more generously with their employees, through salaries, good health care, and pension plans. My late childhood was affected by the protests against the Vietnam War and the general 1960s' expansion of consciousness, all of which I could observe from a certain distance. Not old enough to personally experience the painfulness of the draft or drugs or discrimination, I instead absorbed the era's more positive messages. It all gave me a sense of hopefulness about the possibilities for change in the world. (In sixth grade, I wore pants to school for several days, joining a protest against the girls' dress code in public schools—and felt the success of getting those rules changed!) My parents were both very liberal, and our family talked about politics a lot at the dinner table, giving me a keen sensitivity to unfairness and injustice. The notion that it was our job to try to make the world at least a little less unfair took deep root. This gave a kind of ferocity, I think, to my searching for how to best spend the "little bag of silver" of my own life, and how, if I were to make theater my profession, I really wanted to do it.

Both my parents grew up during the Depression, and through their storytelling I was very aware that the material comforts I enjoyed were not part of their childhoods, although they also conveyed that they had been happy enough without having so much. My father always liked to remind me that before World War II, America was pretty much a third-world country, with most of its population living in rural poverty. But he also stressed that because most people were in the same boat, it didn't seem to matter all that much, especially as a child. These stories, along with the anti-materialism that sprung up in the sixties, gave me a strong sense that there was happiness beyond material things and, indeed, that too many things could actually get in the way of happiness. My father in those times was able to save up enough by working as a lawyer at an insurance company to send me to an Ivy League school without taking on any debt (tuition at the time was around five thousand dollars). It was still a time when college was not only affordable for the middle class but seen as a place to learn and explore, rather than to acquire specific training for specific employment.

And in my after-college years in the early eighties, I continued in what now seems like a luxurious bubble of exploring and not knowing. I headed out to San Francisco with the sense that it was okay to take some time to really try to figure out exactly what my passion might be. I worked in coffee shops and restaurants and a nursery school, I got a job as a government-paid CETA puppeteer at the elementary school in Haight-Ashbury. Most of the hippies were gone from the neighborhood by then, but the city still afforded a leisurely sense of openness and questioning. I was able to patch together ways to support myself, paying my quite manageable rent, and I never felt the need to rush toward leading a life that would bring bigger bills. As I wandered from job to job, I read all I could by Peter Brook and Grotowski and Artaud and Joseph Chaikin, people who asked big questions about the possibilities of theater. I am so grateful that the culture back then permitted me this time for searching. Four years later, I went to graduate directing school in Los Angeles, in large part because the school paid my way. I don't need to say too much about graduate school except that I came away with at least a very clear sense of what kind of theater I *didn't* want to make.

In addition to noticing how many people theater excluded, I sensed that so many people who actually did come to theater didn't want to be there. Especially in Los Angeles. Many came out of a sense of obligation—they'd been invited by acquaintances in the cast who were desperate to be seen by people in the TV and film industry or who were just desperate for an audience. These people had seen lots of theater before and kept their distance. They liked to judge: how did this interpretation compare to others they had seen; how interesting was the set concept, how authentic was the dialogue, how good was the lighting design, how striking were the costumes? But they didn't seem moved by the story. If you could see such people's "theater bodies," I imagined, they would be bloated and fat because they had seen so much theater already. No one seemed hungry for the actual story.

When I thought about doing *The Good Person of Szechwan*, I really didn't want to do it for audiences like that. I loved the story too much. I loved how the play, told from the rare point of view of a female character, paid attention to something I hadn't really seen onstage before: our fundamental human urge to be kind. I loved the way the play explored, with so much humor and irony, how hard it is to act on this deep desire to help others, particularly in our very materialistic world. It acknowledged the profound ache that comes from having to shut down your kindness when the large systems around you force you to use all your energy just to survive. I didn't think the audiences I knew would let themselves care enough about all this. I didn't want them to sit there and judge the production values, missing altogether the way the story could connect with their lives. This really is the core of everything that followed: I just wanted to find an audience who loved the play as much as I did, an audience for whom the story really mattered.

In the play, Shen Te lives in a shack in the poorest part of the city, where she earns a meager living as a prostitute. She gets the bag of silver from three gods who visit her in disguise, as a reward for her kindness in giving them shelter for the night when no one else would. They instruct her to use the money to "be good." Most of the play is about Shen Te trying to help out her poor friends and neighbors but becoming overwhelmed by the enormous difficulty of it all. Their needs are so vast, their demands so endless, her little bag so small. And she needs to take care of herself—and, later, her child—at the same time.

Who else would really *care* about this story? Was there an audience who would really, truly understand the depth and desperation of Shen Te's struggle

ALL THE LIGHTS ON

to be good? At one point she explodes, "How can I be good when everything is so expensive!" The response of mild chuckles from the comfortable audiences I knew would be about the "difficulty" of choosing between writing a hundred-dollar check to a charity or going out to dinner at a nice restaurant. For most of us with a middle-class existence, being taken advantage of when trying to "do good" is inconvenient and sometimes frustrating, but it doesn't leave us tottering on the brink of survival, like everyone in Shen Te's world. It would be very different to watch the play, I imagined, if you were also truly living on the edge, knowing that if you give away a bowl of rice, it could be the last you'd have for many days. "Expensive" would have a very different meaning.

Thinking about an audience of people struggling daily just to survive suddenly opened up all kinds of new questions about the play. I had to admit there was probably a lot that I didn't understand, either: yes, I was barely getting by month to month with my temp jobs, trying to be a theater artist, living in an ugly little rental duplex, but should something go terribly wrong, in the back of my mind I knew that my middle-class parents in Des Moines would always be able to help. The knowledge of that safety net allowed me to take some risks. The value of this net should not be underestimated.

So I became deeply curious to know what an audience without any cushion at all would make of Shen Te's struggles. Did they have the same ones? Would they share her sincere desire to help others? And recognize the way this desire was always getting trampled on, often by the very need and greediness of those she wanted to help? In my little living room in Venice, California, one afternoon, I gathered together a group of talented actor friends, some from grad school, all anxious to practice their craft. All of us shared a sense that theater was leaving a lot of people out. I think most theater artists actually share this ache at some level. My friends agreed that these were worthy questions and that we should take the play, jump in, and try to connect.

But we couldn't imagine how to get such an audience to come to the theater. The forces against it felt enormous: there was the ticket price of course, but also the fact that this audience, like my grandpa, probably wouldn't feel comfortable. Seeing it through their eyes, the theater "scene" felt daunting: people were all dressed up, they'd been to college, they knew some mysterious code of behavior that told them when to applaud and when to be quiet. The plush lobby and seats seemed foreign and unwelcoming. My audience would never come. I realized the only way to reach my imagined, caring audience would be to go to them.

It was 1989, and the sunny beach communities of Venice and Santa Monica were full of people who could not provide for themselves, including many of the mentally ill that Reagan administration policies had turned out of group homes and onto the streets. A homeless shelter might provide us with an audience who could relate to the struggles of the play. I found a drop-in center on an unglamorous stretch of warehouses near the freeway. The center didn't have beds, but it did offer a safe place to hang out during the day, along with some social services and a cup of coffee. It had a noisy central room with worn blue carpet, surrounded by a balcony of little offices buzzing with loud voices and ringing phones. When I approached a staff member and offered a performance of a play by Bertolt Brecht, she seemed puzzled and too busy and harried to think about it very much. However, she said I could put up some flyers announcing a date and time.

We set to work. Seven excellent actors but playing thirty-five characters. A play more than two hours long, plus an intermission. We were anxious, to say the least. What would our audience think? Would they stay with the complicated plot, follow all the character changes? More important, could we bring enough truth to what we were doing to make them want to stay and watch the whole thing? Most daunting of all—how could we of the middle class possibly think that we had anything to say about poverty to people who lived with it every day? We were, at least, an ethnically inclusive group that included an African American, Asian American, Hispanic American, and several European Americans, plus an Australian (it isn't hard to assemble a diverse cast in Los Angeles!). Still, the gulf between our life experiences and those of our audience felt huge.

As we rehearsed, we kept wondering about these homeless people, trying to imagine how they might see things. Our wondering informed the choices we made in rehearsal. We weren't trying to be "original" or "innovative." We weren't thinking about how brilliant choices might enhance our careers or please the critics. We were just trying to figure out how we could best tell the story so that people would connect it with their lives.

One thing I vowed—we would not have the slightest whiff of condescension to our work. I imagined that people in shelters were always getting preached to: "Here's what's wrong with you; here's how you can improve yourself; here's how you can solve your problems. You probably won't be able to understand anything difficult, so we'll keep it really simple. We know how to help you; let us help you so we can feel better about ourselves." We approached our audience with enormous respect for their hard-won life experiences. It wasn't difficult. One step inside a shelter and humility is pretty inescapable.

Although the play takes place in a slum, it felt very important to stress that this was a "fairy tale" world and not a realistic depiction of poverty. I wanted to be very clear from the start that we were not going to try to pretend to be experts in those physical details. It seemed essential to make up a world, set in another time and another place, where no one could be an expert. Imaginative distance was crucial. Because the script had so much humor and irony, it seemed that whatever set we made should be playful, too.

We didn't have any money. But here that invisible safety net of a middle-class family—and a caring, supportive parent—came into play. I got my own little bag of silver from my mother without even asking: five hundred dollars to pay for the set. It felt wrong not to pay my actor friends for their hard work, and I vowed this would be the last time that ever happened. But it was a start.

We bought fabric and dye and paint. I was thinking of the colors of the sunset on the beach, where many homeless people spent a lot of time. We dyed cloth and cut out shapes to hang on a clothesline—red and pink doors, yellow shop windows, purple and orange trees, green factory signs. We set four poles in small cardboard barrels to form the four corners of our little stage and stretched rope between to hang the cutouts on with clothespins. We filled plastic shopping bags with sand from the beach to weigh down the poles in their barrels, making sure they would stand up. It took a lot of heavy bags, so everyone had to carry piles of them in their car trunks. Then just a few boards for benches and shelves, a bowl of rice, some cigars made from cardboard tubes, not too much else. We rehearsed over several months, whenever we could find spare time.

On the afternoon of the performance, I remember shouting across the parking lot of the shelter to greet the actress playing Shen Te, Christi Mays, both of us lugging our bags of sand. Though we were smiling, we were terrified. My head was pounding: "What are you doing? This is going to be a disaster. Why are you doing a play here? This is absolutely ridiculous. They are going to think you're stupid and weird and laugh in your face; they're going to hate it. Put the sand bags back in the trunk and get out of here." It was my first experience of a moment that has happened at least once in every single production since: a sharp, clear realization, like the chime of a bell, that I am out of my mind. But as also always happens, the energy of sheer necessity took over: we'd said we'd do the show, we'd rehearsed it, the actors were arriving with costumes and set pieces, of course we had to go ahead and do it.

We walked into the space. Sunshine streamed through the windows—the beautiful weather outside seemed much more tempting than the prospect of staying inside to watch some little play. There actually weren't very many homeless people around: a weathered-looking young man wrapped in a blanket, a few women with shopping bags, a group of older black men in the corner drinking coffee. But we set up the poles, tied a rope between the back two, and stretched a purple cloth between the front two to make a curtain, using paper clips for hooks. We had brought extra cardboard barrels and boards and used them to make little benches for the audience, setting them up hopefully in front of the stage.

It didn't seem that anyone had noticed the flyers. No one—including the staff—seemed to have any idea that we were doing a Brecht play there that afternoon. The mood in the room among the twenty or so homeless people ranged from skepticism to puzzlement to complete indifference as we put up the set. It felt like a ridiculous place to attempt to perform a two-and-a-half-hour play. My "you've got to be out of your mind" chime kept getting louder.

We'd photocopied some programs, so I went around the room offering them, inviting people to take a seat on a bench and try the play out. Most people just looked at me suspiciously. Finally one or two women reluctantly moved over to the benches; a minute or two later, a few more followed. Most still hung back, arms folded, probably in anticipation of a blast of condescension headed their way from the "do-gooders."

We began. Wang the Water Seller came out in front of his sewer pipe home, painted on the purple curtain, to sing about how hard it is to sell water when it's raining. We wrote the song to be very minimal, half-spoken, anticipating how strange the idea of someone just starting to sing in the middle of such a room might be, but it still seemed very strange. The audience kept their distance. The three flimsily disguised gods entered, demanding that Wang find them lodging for the night. I sensed a slight tension in the room and felt myself go on alert: of course, any presentation of "gods" onstage smelled of trouble—was this weary audience worried we might be trying to preach to them about how to be good?

The three gods: Bill Burns, Craig Fernandez, Marilyn Henkus, *The Good Person of Szechwan*, Venice soup kitchen, 1990.

When Shen Te answered her door, I thought I sensed another tiny audience shift. Shen Te was known throughout the slum for her kind heart, but one look at the gods and she responded with the same suspicion the audience was feeling; she indicated she was not particularly interested in pleasing such ridiculous beings. She finally agreed, with more than a little reluctance, to put them up, but only out of loyalty to her good friend Wang, who was terrified of what the gods might do if he failed to find them a room. The audience seemed to be paying a little more attention; perhaps they were approving of Shen Te's honesty?

Finally, about ten minutes into the play, we got a signal from the audience that they were connecting. The gods were showering Shen Te with praise for her good deed, proclaiming her the last truly good person on earth, when she interrupted them with a very inconvenient fact of her life: she sold herself for a living. "I'd like to keep the commandments, to honor my mother and father and always tell the truth," she protested. "I'd be overjoyed not to covet my neighbor's house, and I'd be delighted to stay with just one man. But how? How is it done? Even by breaking a few commandments, I barely get by. How can I be good when everything is so expensive?" The second god responded sharply, "There's nothing we can do about that. We never meddle in economics." At this moment, there was a chuckle. A few more, and then a guffaw from the back. The audience began to catch on that we were not on the side of the gods and their endless exhortations to "be good." The play was on Shen Te's side—and on their side. We were not going to lecture them, like the gods, and tell them how to be better.

That first little chuckle was a whiff of cool ocean air, allowing us all a big internal sigh of relief. Someone was connecting, perhaps in spite of herself, someone was deciding to open up to the strange event occurring in this very unlikely place. The skepticism had started to melt away. When the gods, after a quick conference, decided to "pay" Shen Te for their lodging, giving her a small bag containing a thousand silver dollars—along with strict instructions to use it to "do good"—her delighted yelps of joy seemed to win over the audience completely. It was a fantasy everyone could relate to, and the audience was with Shen Te for the rest of the ride.

Their pleasure in Shen Te continued as she used the money to buy her own tobacco shop. They seemed also to approve wholeheartedly when Shen Te, overwhelmed by the need and greediness of her neighbors in the slum, found she had to create an alter ego for herself, a "cousin," the ruthless businessman Mr. Shui Ta. Donning a hat and suit coat and lowering her voice, she kicked the neighbors out and order was restored. The audience shifted back and forth easily with Shen Te between her two personas, the kind-hearted one and the ruthless one, and began to vocalize their approval. At one point, dressed as Mr. Shui Ta, Shen Te turned away in the middle of making a deal and took off her bowler hat to exclaim, "I am horrified to see how much luck is needed to keep from being crushed! How many brilliant ideas! How many good friends!" The audience responded with murmurs of support, "Uh-huh!" and "You got that right!" Mr. Shui Ta then turned back to seal the deal with a cigar, and Christi, the actress playing him, quietly glowed from the support her character had just received.

At other points the listening became very intense and focused, as when Shen Te sat on a park bench with a young pilot who had tried to hang himself because he hadn't been able to come up with a bribe to get a flying license. She told a story of a crane with a broken wing she had known as a child. The crane was good natured but got very restless in the spring and fall when big flocks of birds flew overhead. The quiet in the room was electric. For a moment there was a shared understanding among thirty people in a homeless shelter, including a janitor and some staff who had paused in their work, of what it feels like to have a broken wing, to be unable to fly.

The vocal responses grew. When Shen Te paused on the way to her wedding to the young pilot to express doubts about whether her groom really loved her or was just after her tobacco shop money, some women in the audience shouted out warnings: "That's right, honey, you stay away from him! He's bad news!" Christi discovered that her "monologue" was actually a conversation with the audience. She spoke her next lines a little more defiantly, "But I want to go with the man I love. I don't want to count the cost. I don't want to think about whether it's right. I don't want to know whether he loves me. I want to go with the man I love!" The women in the audience shifted their sympathies once again. "Yes. Yes. Mmmm-hmmm. You go girl," they murmured in knowing, supportive tones. I was speechless with surprise and delight, and I knew that Christi was, too. This audience had no problem completely embracing both sides.

We were also surprised by responses we had not imagined. At one point, Shen Te was outside hanging up her laundry, having decided not to go through with her marriage. As she bent over her basket, she suddenly felt a little dizzy. There was a quiet chorus of "uh-ohs." The audience instantly knew. No words needed. A baby was coming. And a baby can bring a lot of trouble when you're living on the edge.

But Shen Te ignored the audience's alarm and went on to express joy at the discovery. She proceeded to take her imagined child on a tour of the neighborhood, holding his little invisible hand, showing him the wonders of the world. I had always greatly loved this part; I had never really seen the anticipation of the delights of having a child expressed so well in a script. But the audience didn't seem to share these feelings quite so much. We were surprised—and informed—by the audience's different response. For many, the pleasant anticipation of a child might be a luxury, outweighed by the difficult realities a single mother would face raising her child in a very harsh world. Though when Shen Te paused in her tour to point out a magnificent cherry tree in a wealthy neighbor's yard, everyone expressed great pleasure and approval as she then taught her imagined child how to steal the cherries!

The reverie ended abruptly when Shen Te stumbled on the sight of an actual child fishing for food in a garbage can. At this moment, her feelings swung back in line with the audience's. Shaken to her core, she determined to change herself back into Mr. Shui Ta one last time, vowing to be good to her child but a wild beast to all others. There seemed to be little question in the audience that Shen Te was doing the right thing by completely giving up any aspiration to do good. The absolute ferocity and ruthlessness needed to protect your child in a brutal, cutthroat world was something everyone clearly understood.

As the play built to a close, the honest and easy shifting of the audience's sympathies continued. They seemed glad to have Mr. Shui Ta (growing ever plumper!) take matters firmly in hand once again and open up a tobacco fac-

The tobacco factory, (left to right) Christianne Mays, Suzanne Kato, Kate Cherry, Bill Burns, Marilyn Henkus, Kenneth Ransom, *The Good Person of Szechwan*, Los Angeles Women's Shelter, 1990.

tory. But they also sided with Shen Te's neighbors, who, with no other jobs around, were forced to work at the factory for extremely low pay. Like the workers, the audience then began to miss Shen Te, who had not been seen for many days. In any case, most seemed pleased with the irony when Mr. Shui Ta was arrested for Shen Te's kidnapping and found himself in court facing a tribunal of three judges who looked suspiciously like the three gods.

I had found myself an audience who deeply understood both sides of Shen Te's very human dilemma, appreciating it with all its pain and humor and irony. Thank goodness Brecht, in ending the play, did not choose a side or offer any easy answers. As Mr. Shui Ta began to remove his coat and tie, revealing to the judges that he was actually the same person as the now quite pregnant Shen Te, he/she cried out the heartbreak the audience understood deeply in their bones:

> *Your order long ago*
> *To be good and yet to live*

Was a thunderbolt:
It has torn me in two halves.
I don't know how it happened
But to be good to others
and to myself at the same time
I could not do it.
Your world is not an easy one, Enlightened Ones! . . .
And yet to give was a passion with me.
A happy face and I walked on clouds.
Condemn me: all my crimes
were committed to help my neighbor,
to love my lover
and to keep my little one from want.
For your great, godly deeds,
I was too poor, so small.

And, of course, to the audience's great relish, the gods, as they had done all along, ignored Shen Te's honesty. "Just be good and everything will turn out all right," they reassured her as they stepped onto a little cluster of rose-colored clouds (cardboard cutouts, of course), hurrying to get back to heaven as quickly as possible. As Shen Te ran after them, she pleaded for the use of her ruthless cousin. The gods paused just long enough to rule that she could be Shui Ta, but only once a month. Then they happily floated away, barely able to hear the last word of the play, a guttural cry from the woman whose belly was swollen with child, *"Help!"*

The gods had left Shen Te—and us—behind, torn in two, without any answers at all.

There was hearty applause from the little audience of thirty. The little audience that remains the biggest one of my life. The actors came out, wild eyed with relief, to take several bows in front of our small purple curtain. They stepped into the audience to mingle.

It had not been a completely smooth ride. During the performance, people sometimes got up to leave. Whenever someone did, our hearts sank: we

ALL THE LIGHTS ON

The Good Person of Szechwan, **curtain call, Venice soup kitchen, 1990.**

were sure they must not have liked the show. In this very intimate performance situation, there was time to make a personal connection with almost every audience member. The older men around the edges of the room would often talk during the play, though sometimes they'd stop to tune in. Social workers would scurry by without even a glance. Phones rang and sometimes the conversations were really loud. One person fell asleep for part of the show (though he did seem to enjoy it again once he woke up).

As the director, standing behind the audience, or sometimes crouching when things got really intense, I experienced the moments of disconnect more keenly than the actors, since I could only watch. For me, it was a stomach-lurching roller coaster ride. At the time, my only explanation for those moments was, "They must not like the show!" Only later would we come to understand that people, no matter how much they might be enjoying a performance, have to leave to meet with their social workers or for a job interview. Or that someone might have been really looking forward to a cup of coffee and the chance to talk to others after a lonely night on the street. Or that drop-in centers often provide the only safe, warm place to sleep, even if it's in the daytime. Even if there's a play going on right in front of you. Life is more important than theater. I understood this intellectually, but it would take me a long time to really absorb it and just be able to relax and let go when such things happened.

But despite all this, we really had succeeded in connecting. Of course, I couldn't tell exactly what was going through any one person's mind. But, as I think any director does observing an audience, I'd put together a narrative from the moments where connection—or the lack of it—was tangible. After the show, the audience was effusive, shaking the actors' hands, praising them, thanking them. We had also put out a little notebook where people could write comments, so I still have some exact words: "I enjoyed this play—boy was it real good!" "Terrific, well-acted out—one of the most funniest performances!" "The most extraordinary performance I've ever seen."

More important, the play had spoken to people's lives. "I think someone wrote my unauthorized biography!" wrote one woman. "It was moving and a release," wrote another, "Wow! It helped me get a new perspective on a lot of difficult things in my life. It was fun and heartful." Opinions on the characters' behavior were offered, including one of my all-time favorites: "I think this dual personality chick should just take the money and say fuck you." And it was very clear that for some, at least, the story truly did matter. As another man wrote, "Things like this make me really want to get my life in order. It makes me see life really has a meaning. Thank you." No, thank *you*, I thought. For this audience anyway, theater was about life, not just aesthetic choices. And they had enabled me to see so clearly that my success as an artist came from having been able to engage and connect, in a deep and meaningful way, with them—with people whom many would think I had little or no connection at all.

The best comment that day came from the janitor standing in the back, pausing to watch whenever he could between chores. He came right up to me and said, "Thank you for treating us like we have brains in our heads." A light from his eyes shone directly into mine. It confirmed all my instincts. At that moment I renewed that vow to always treat my audiences with the utmost respect—for their intelligence, for their imaginations, and for their hard-won life experiences. This would always be my starting point.

ALL THE LIGHTS ON

That very same janitor made another comment that afternoon that confirmed our intuitions about how we approached Brecht. He presented us with another discovery when he said, "I liked how you could sit back and think about what was going on at the same time you were really enjoying the story." The audience had thought about the story as they watched it, commenting on it as it went on. And all just because it was there in the writing. At certain moments, Brecht simply had a character turn to the audience and ask them what they thought about the situation. This audience answered back, offering their opinions out loud. The "alienation effect." That's really all it took. There was no need for special acting techniques or angular movements or pale makeup. Just characters who directly asked the audience questions—and an audience unafraid to answer back. It was the first of many, many discoveries that our first-time audiences would help us make.

And now, more than twenty years later, here I am. Here is Minneapolis. Soon after my daughter was born, my then husband and I moved from Los Angeles to Minneapolis. Another city with a large pool of very talented actors, but one with deeply committed theatergoers, arts advocates, and philanthropists as well. A place where the unequal distribution of wealth seems a little less severe. Here I have raised my daughter and a theater company. Through an inexplicable process of groping and stumbling, listening and focusing, lugging large objects up stairways and down hallways, plus bumping into both lucky good fortune and the bounteous generosity and kindnesses of so many, we have made a theater company. Ten Thousand Things brings the best possible theater, plays of Shakespeare and Aeschylus and Beckett, to audiences who have seen little of it before, those in prisons and shelters and adult education centers and rural towns and housing projects and Indian reservations and chemical dependency treatment centers, as well as to enthusiastic veteran theatergoers in consistently sold-out performances for the general public, all performed in large bare rooms, with no stage, just right on the floor inside a small circle of folding chairs, with all the fluorescent lights in the room turned on. Our budget is modest, we don't need our own building, our set supply budget is little more than that of our very first show, but we pay our highly skilled artists on a par with the largest theater companies in town.

We have even become Johnny Appleseeds of a sort, taking this unique model to other theaters around the country who are also eager to find ways to reach outside their buildings with excellent work. And all along this journey, the honest, openhearted encounters of our first-time audiences with our first-rate artists have led us to make wonderful discoveries about theater—pinpointing just what makes it thrive and flourish.

But as I dragged the rattling poles back to my hatchback, I couldn't possibly understand the implications of what had just happened. What I did know for certain then was that this audience who had seen little if any theater before, who did not take it for granted, had opened their hearts to us—and to the story. They allowed the play to resonate with their very lives. They had actually given us more than we had given them. They gave us delight and amazement and affirmation through the support and encouragement and advice they had offered to the characters during the play. And they also gave us new depths of understanding into the play itself. These were all people who lived on the edge financially, every day, just like Shen Te. They understood, in a way a paying audience simply couldn't, the enormous difficulty and risk of Shen Te's efforts to do good. They had made us aware, through their imagined presence in rehearsals and their actual presence during the show, of the high stakes involved in every choice and decision Shen Te has to make. And by opening their hearts to us, they had allowed us to connect with people we had somehow been taught to think we might have nothing in common with at all.

One last thing I did know then, as I swung the last sandbag into the trunk, was that I was going to have to do this again.

ALL THE LIGHTS ON

RADIANCE
The Heart

THAT VERY FIRST CHUCKLE from the audience in the Santa Monica shelter was a tiny burst of treasure that I have been searching ardently for more of ever since. The chuckle was a sign that we as theater artists somehow had emitted something that had touched one homeless woman's experience of the world; her small breath of laughter had in turn fed us, easing our enormous insecurity that we might fail to touch on anything we had in common. As the performance went on, the audience began to trust us still more, letting down their guard, first murmuring and then talking to the characters; they encouraged the actors to adjust and deepen, and then to reach further out and try for more. The energies that were released and exchanged grew, until at times it seemed like small suns within each of us had been uncovered.

THE PURSUIT OF RADIANCE This ineffable feeling of deep exchange with an audience is one I would venture to say most theater practitioners long for yet do not experience as often as they would like in their careers. I've just recently thought of a name for these bursts, which come from humans sharing with each other, even for just a moment, their most profound and honest selves: *radiance*. Radiance is more than a "connection," which suggests energy flowing just two ways, back and forth, from actor to audience and back again. Because radiance comes from such a deep place, with minds, hearts, and imaginations all engaged at once, it spills out into the world in all directions, in surprising and unexpected ways. Theater is uniquely suited to create radiance because of its collective aliveness, because we meet in one space and imagine new worlds together in the moment.

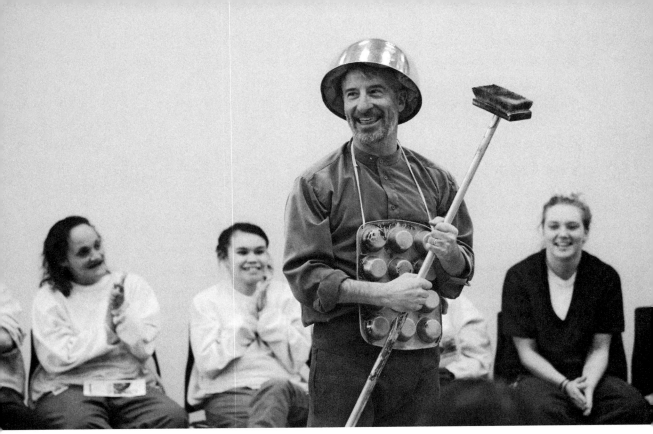

**Steven Epp, *Man
of La Mancha*,
women's correc-
tional facility,
2011.**

The pursuit of radiance has shaped everything I've done at Ten Thousand
Things. I loved the first experience of it so much that I wanted to figure out
everything else I could possibly do to encourage it. My thirst for radiance
came, of course, from wanting people to be blown away by their very first encounter with theater. But it also came from craving the way our work as artists was clarified and deepened by the audiences' refreshing responses. For
many years, I was compelled to sit and watch each and every performance
from beginning to end, observing the audience and the actors intently, obses-
sively, hoping for moments of engagement, basking in them if they happened,
writhing in quiet agony if there was confusion or disinterest instead. Every
moment got etched into my being, and all the way through each tour I worked
on figuring out how we could make it work better.

And, yet, as ineffable as radiance is, I believe there are many factors that are in fact quite technical that can help to foster it. Going to the "regular" theater, where I very rarely felt this quality, I began to notice so many obstacles and barriers that were put in the way. I began to realize that a lot of what Ten Thousand Things did to increase radiance was simply to remove those obstacles and barriers. If a small sun is hidden in each of us, then a big part of allowing it to shine comes from taking away whatever keeps it hidden.

BARRIERS TO RADIANCE   Many of the barriers to radiance are physical. When we removed them, we did so without really thinking about it. We removed them because we had to. Because Ten Thousand Things goes directly to its audiences, instead of expecting them to come to us, we had to make do without a lot of "necessities."

Stages, for example. To reach our audiences, wherever they might be, we created the play so that we only needed a large room and some chairs. Insisting on a stage would have drastically limited the number of places we could perform. Once, early on, we happened to perform in a church space that had a small stage, so we thought we might as well use it. We were doing the seventeenth-century Spanish drama *Life's a Dream* by Pedro Calderón de la Barca. We discovered, oh so painfully, that the distance that stage created between us and the audience, with the actors raised up on a platform, was deadly. The audience of inner-city high school kids was restless and bored with a story that had been riveting to other groups of youth at risk. We realized it was *necessary* to be on the same level as our audience, just a few feet or, even better, just a few inches away. Certainly never more than three rows back. The distance presented by a stage was just too big an obstacle for us to overcome.

We didn't bring lighting instruments along, of course; we just turned on whatever fluorescent lights were in the room. Again, we didn't think much about it; it's just what we had to do. It wasn't until about our seventh production that an actress, standing on the sidelines waiting to go on, whispered to me, "I just love how we can see the audience!" I started with surprise—this had never occurred to me before. I was flooded with all the ramifications of this obvious fact. The actors could see the audience all the time, onstage or off, and so could receive every detail of their reactions full force, fine-tuning and adjusting all the while. And of course all those lights explained both my ability to make such detailed observations of the audience and the intensity of my elation and agony—greater, I think, than when a director sits in the back row of a dark house, only able to listen to a muffled audience. Dark houses, we discovered, actually dimmed the intensity of the exchange between audience and actors. We were much better off without them.

MAKING THINGS UP TOGETHER   We began to see how our inability to have elaborate sets and oodles of props boosted the intensity of our work. Personally, I had always preferred empty stages, with lots of spaces for imagination to fill in; I intuited that this was how theater worked best. But now we were entering places where people were without expectations and used to making do with very little, where the rooms we had to perform in were already very spare—cinderblock walls, linoleum floors, maybe industrial carpeting. As we held up a Hula-Hoop and asked the audience to imagine it was the moon, we could viscerally feel the pleasure they took in the invitation. They would giggle, resisting for a bit, of course, but then take the plunge. We were offering them a chance to exercise the muscles of their imaginations and participate in the creation of an escape from their barren surroundings, at least for a few hours. We were helping them remember that they could still pretend, just like kids do. There is a palpable energy when everyone in a room is making things up together. It most definitely adds to radiance.

NEGLECTED STORYTELLING   Many of the barriers we concentrated on removing were not physical ones. All the moments where the story wasn't clear. Or where there was a lack of urgency in what was happening onstage. Or where actors were not reaching out to directly connect with the audience right in front of their noses. Those were moments I could "fix" myself, as a director. Quite honestly, I mostly wanted to eliminate the pain I felt whenever first-time audiences didn't connect, when they became restless, or when it seemed we were actually confirming, even for a moment, their suspicions that theater was boring after all. I didn't want to have to sit through any more experiences of that. My directing muscles actually got quite a workout, since

I had very few tools beyond actors' bodies, sound, and the text. But any time the story was clear and urgent and lively, I noticed most of the audience leaning forward, so I kept trying everything within my power to make them lean forward all the time.

AUDIENCE RESISTANCE   As we were noticing how certain physical "requirements" for theater actually got in the way, we were also encountering the enormous barriers presented by the initial attitudes of our audience members. We had sort of guessed, but didn't fully understand until we started, that most people who have never seen theater before really *don't want* to see it. So many have picked up the impression that it's just for rich people who have college degrees, that it's boring and hard to understand. The audiences we encounter can be defensive at first, and this sometimes comes off as contempt. I remember one homeless woman who, upon walking into a shelter and seeing our

Audience at women's correctional facility, *The Good Person of Szechwan*, 2005.

little setup, exclaimed, "I don't wanna see no Shakespeare shit!" She turned right back around and exited out the door. (We weren't actually doing Shakespeare that time.) On top of these learned attitudes, there was also usually well-founded suspicion and distrust of strangers who came into their space: so often they were just "do-gooders" who wanted to feel better about themselves by "helping." As we began almost every show, we had to confront these very thick walls of suspicion, contempt, and indifference head on. As performers, we had no choice but to learn to blast right through it with the only tools we had—honesty, humility, focus, and playfulness. Such attitudes took audiences by surprise. Over all these years, I have come to greatly appreciate the enormous importance of the element of surprise in cracking through people's barriers. Almost always, after ten minutes or so of strong doses of these unexpected demonstrations of respect toward people who are usually afforded so little of it, the walls started to fall. Radiance would start to seep through.

Now, more than twenty years in, half of the performances we do are for members of the paying public, always in the exact same bare-bones manner in which we perform for our other audiences. I want to be very clear that audiences who pay for their tickets and have seen a lot of theater also put up barriers. Indeed, their attitudes were the very barriers that had moved me to seek other audiences in the first place. Quite honestly, we almost always find that the walls of judgment and critical distance erected by experienced theatergoers are much harder to blast through than anything nontraditional audiences offer. And yet, all the ways we've had to shape our theater in order to reach first-time audiences—focus on clarity, urgency, depth, and honesty, with no darkness in which to hide, plus insistence on all imaginations having to work full throttle—all this has also worked to shake up those jaded paying audiences. We surprise them, too. Eventually (though it usually takes about thirty minutes instead of ten), we are able to break through the walls put up by people with wealth and watch them begin to allow their own radiance to burst through.

Here, I'd like to highlight the potential for radiance that all people bring with them to the meeting place of the theater. While I truly believe all humans have light inside them, at Ten Thousand Things we've noticed over the years

ALL THE LIGHTS ON

Luverne Seifert and Jim Licht-scheidl, *At Your Service* by Kevin Kling, at Open Book, performing for a traditional audience, 2004.

that some people just seem to have easier access to this light. With many of our nontraditional audiences, despite all the hardships they've experienced, there is not as much "crust" to remove. In a funny way, both Ten Thousand Things actors and nontraditional audiences have a radiance that is perhaps a little closer to the surface than usual. (I've also noticed that over time the veteran theatergoers who keep returning to our barebones performances seem to have easier access to that radiance as well.)

The theatrical work we do also attracts a certain kind of artist. It doesn't really appeal to people who are primarily interested in bolstering their résumés and advancing in their careers. Indeed, many actors have told me that our work provides a welcome relief from those kinds of pressures because it calls on something much more powerful: a desire to reach out for something bigger than oneself, to find a way to connect with other humans who on the surface appear very different. I think the work actually attracts, if I may call them this, radiant artists. Artists with easy access to the honesty, humility, humor, and generosity that are necessary to break through audience barriers.

H. Adam Harris
and Sun Mee
Chomet, *Dirt
Sticks* by Kira
Obolensky,
Avalon School,
2014.

And our audiences in prisons and shelters, in turn, often bring that same kind of easy access to the radiance in their beings—once we have earned their trust. To be treated with respect for their intelligence, imaginations, and life experience is rare—and when it actually happens, they permit their radiance to burst through. They have often experienced a long drought of respect, and once they feel it, they are eager to give back in return.

Of course, every good theater performance in any venue can bring about connections and exchanges between actors and audience. But the extremes of our performance conditions can cause an intensity so strong, a connection that feels so immediate and charged that I think radiance occurs more often. Truthfully, I haven't experienced a lot of radiance in much theater I've

ALL THE LIGHTS ON

attended in buildings where we sit far away in the dark, watching a story unfold on a stage laden with detailed sets that fill in every empty space with every conceivable prop to make things easier on our imaginations. There *is* radiance sometimes, to be sure—but I think more of it in theater couldn't hurt.

In the chapters that follow, I want to share in more detail the discoveries we've made about what creates more radiant theater. As I talk about these discoveries, I'll follow a path that roughly corresponds to the way a production is created and born—through the first imaginings of an audience, the choice of a play, the imagining of production values, rehearsing, and performing. I also want to discuss the political consequences of this way of doing theater in the big world, as well as describe the organization that has organically emerged to support this work. I hope simply to spark your own questionings of theater

Storm-tossed ship at sea, *The Tempest*, Hubbs Center for Lifelong Learning, 1999.

today and encourage your own reimagining of how else it might be. I hope you will take for yourself anything you find provocative, inspiring, or useful and ignore anything you don't.

Most of these discoveries were made through absolute necessity. They were made because of the inescapable conditions that come as part of wanting to connect plays to audiences who might find their stories urgent. Indeed, it strikes me that theater is perhaps at its most radiant when everything about it is utterly necessary. When there is nothing that is superfluous. I think of the simple circle of chairs in which we perform, with actors and rings of audience radiating their energies from the center. I see it from an aerial view. While this book is in no way meant to be an argument to urge others to do theater exactly the way we do it, I start to zoom out, getting a view of people pulling up chairs to make other small circles in other places, each generating their own light, dotting the land with small radiant fires. It does seem like something we could use more of.

ALL THE LIGHTS ON

2

IMAGINING THE AUDIENCE, RIGHT OR WRONG
Beginnings

IN MY TWENTIES, I had my first "professional" job, assisting a famous director at a large theater in Los Angeles. We were working on a new play, and the two of us seemed to have a fun, easygoing rapport. I commented once during rehearsals, "Oh, the audience will probably really like this part." The director snapped back at me, "How do you know? You can't ever predict what an audience will like or how they will respond! Don't even try."

This harsh admonition to leave the audience out of it startled me. Of course, in one way he was right: you can't ever predict how an audience will respond, and if you try, you'll most likely be wrong. But at the time I was in the middle of trying to prepare for our first *Good Person* rehearsals, working on the script in my free time between the assistant directing job and another job as a proofreader. As I read the play, I felt absolutely compelled to try to imagine the responses of the audience of homeless people, whose experiences of life were probably different from mine in many ways. Even though I knew I might be wrong in my imagining, I just felt I had to try. I didn't want to risk selling short the experiences of people who had lived very hard lives. I wanted to be absolutely sure we connected with them. I wanted them to be hit by truth in their first contact with theater, perhaps even experience joy from seeing their truth reflected by others onstage. Necessity dictated that I try to imagine how the audience might see things. To avoid doing so felt arrogant and foolish.

I've come to see that this simple action—of consciously imagining how an audience might see the events and characters in a play—is actually not common in most of our theaters. For example, when inviting directors to work with

**Maggie Chestovich
and Kiseung Rhee,
Life's a Dream,
Dorothy Day
Center, 2010.**

the company, I always ask them to propose their own projects—I want them to work on plays they personally find compelling. But I am always surprised at how often their proposals stop with their own enthusiasm for a script. I often have to prod them to take the next step: "But why would anyone else want to watch this?" And of course, with Ten Thousand Things, the word "anyone" has the force of its full meaning: immigrants and the homeless and inmates as well as seasoned theatergoers, encompassing almost all ethnicities and income levels. Many directors report that they've never really thought about this question before. The assumption seems to be that if the *artist* finds a play compelling, that's enough. If an artist is interested, an audience will be, too.

ALL THE LIGHTS ON

FEARS AND HAZARDS   Of course, imagining the answer to the question, "Why would anyone *else* want to watch this?" contains some hazards. It requires that you make some assumptions about a group of people, and that could lead to errors and even stereotyping. But I would argue very strongly that the real danger lies in *not* trying to imagine the audience. When you *don't* try to imagine them, you are making assumptions about them anyway—*without being aware of it*. Most likely you're assuming that the audience will be the people who usually do come to theater—white, upper-middle-class, and over fifty. And this group of people, speaking in broad strokes, has a specific set of circumstances that informs their perceptions. They are sitting on a cushion of wealth. So this means some things are more important or interesting to them than to people who do not have such cushions. Such financially comfortable people are actually a very small fraction of the human population. And yet that is to whom most of our theater, without really being aware of it, is shaped to speak. We assume that everyone is like this small segment. It's no wonder so many people don't bother to go to theater.

The fear of making assumptions about an audience is understandable; on one level, it does seem ridiculous to try. You can't possibly know the astonishing variety of specific experiences of individuals in any group. And of course, as we all know, the responses of each audience depend on so many intangibles. The day of the week, for example: Friday-night audiences are often quieter, perhaps because everyone has just finished the workweek and is tired; Saturday-night audiences are often louder and livelier. And yet, just now, in talking about Fridays and Saturdays, I've made assumptions. These assumptions turn out to be correct, more often than not. Of course we've all experienced a lively Friday-night crowd and a quiet Saturday crowd—there are always exceptions and mistakes. But we seem to need to make assumptions anyway. We seem compelled to lump each audience together and talk of it as one being. Why?

A CONVERSATION WITH THE AUDIENCE   Because theater is at heart a conversation. When you talk to someone, you're always trying to imagine what is going on inside their heads, since you can't see their actual thoughts. You scan their faces for twitches, listen to the intensity of their breath, their tones, inflections, and pauses, searching far beyond just the content of the words they use to reply. Using all the visual and aural cues you have, you still can't exactly know what's really going on inside—so you make assumptions. As theater artists, we do this all the time in performance: if most of the audience seemed to laugh at a particular line on a particular night, an actor adjusts his next line accordingly, even if not every person was laughing. And after that particular performance, we talk about the experience of it by grouping the audience together as one animal: "Boy that was a lively crowd tonight; they really liked it!"—even though many people in the audience might not have been laughing or enjoying the play at all.

Similarly, when you prepare for an important conversation, you use all the information you have about your intended listener to try to imagine how they might respond, to help you plan what to say and how best to say it. You make assumptions based on whatever you know of their experiences. Sometimes those assumptions are correct and the conversation goes smoothly—and sometimes the assumptions are wrong, and the listener explodes with a response you couldn't possibly have imagined. So you jump around and readjust. That's how it goes. Making assumptions about your listener is an absolutely essential and inescapable part of preparing for any conversation. So why wouldn't we do this when preparing to perform a play?

ONE-TO-ONE MATCHING   After that first production of *The Good Person of Szechwan* for the homeless shelter in Los Angeles, I continued to try to match a play to a specific audience. Our next endeavor, *Electra* by Sophocles, I matched, somewhat obviously, to girls in juvenile prison. I imagined they might also share Electra's experience of being deeply betrayed and craving revenge. This simple match up of main character to specific audience worked well, so I continued the process: Calderón's *Life's a Dream*, a seventeenth-century Spanish drama about a prince whom the stars predict will grow up a monster, suggested audiences of youth at risk. *Mud* by María Irene Fornés, about a rural woman struggling to learn to read while supporting her very dependent brother, suggested audiences of adult literacy students.

ALL THE LIGHTS ON

But then it started to become clear that we needed to reach beyond these easy one-to-one match ups. For one thing, there weren't that many juvenile correctional facilities or adult literacy centers in our area to support an entire tour. The actors needed more performances to give them a chance to really dig in, and after putting in so much rehearsal time, I wanted more people to see each show. I began to see I could become more universal in my imagining, that the stories we told had large struggles that could appeal to all kinds of marginalized audiences as well as paying ones. Inmates would of course have a strong sense of imprisonment and confinement as well as an experience of the justice system and how it feels to be judged. Elderly people in nursing homes could probably relate to experiences of confinement and judgment as well, in addition to feelings of abandonment. And many inmates would probably deeply understand what it feels like to be abandoned; homeless people might also, or those in chemical dependency treatment centers. The process of looking at stories through the eyes of different groups of people revealed for me the common struggles that we as human beings *all* share.

A MULTIPLICITY OF AUDIENCES   Our audiences now have broadened beyond homeless shelters to include an array of groups of people living on the edge—inmates, immigrants, the elderly, youth at risk, people in psychiatric hospitals, women in chemical dependency treatment, students at tribal colleges. Each time we add a new group to a tour, I feel compelled to try to reach out to imagine them, though my imaginings are admittedly very rough and often based in ignorance. I use just a very few broad brushstrokes to help me try to understand how they might perceive the play. My brushstrokes come from making one or two assumptions about experiences that they probably share, based on a few obvious factual circumstances of their lives. Low-income people, for example, do not have access to much money. That simple fact affects how they experience the world. I try to imagine how they might see certain moments, certain characters, certain scenes. And as I try to see the play through their eyes, some moments become more important. I feel new empathy for certain characters that I might have been more dismissive of before. It feels more important than ever to give all characters equal weight and compassion and create a level playing field. The stakes of almost everything that happens in the story become much higher. New possibilities, new choices open up to me, as I imagine audiences different from the one we are all most accustomed to.

A TREASURE CHEST OF LENSES   The kind of imagining of audience groups we do as artists at Ten Thousand Things is quite different from the act of thinking in stereotypes. Our imagining centers on the possible *shared experiences* of a group of people. Unlike stereotypes, these assumptions have nothing to do with people's intelligence, imagination, sensitivity, or worth as human beings. In fact, with our artistic work, we shatter such hurtful stereotypes: we assume from the beginning that marginalized people have enormous quantities of all these positive qualities. But we need a place to begin the conversation. So I start by imagining through a lens constructed from a few inescapable facts of a group's economic and physical circumstances. This new lens can, in turn, offer startling new perspectives on well-worn theatrical territory and become a wellspring of creative ideas.

Indeed, as the wildly different groups we took each play to expanded, I found myself collecting a treasure chest of different lenses, which has truly become a fantastic source of wealth for me as an artist. As we returned again and again to certain venues, to juvenile facilities or immigrant centers or veterans' homes, certain general characteristics of each audience became clearer, and the basis on which we made our assumptions became more grounded in actual experience. As the array of audiences we performed for grew, the conversations I had in my head with different groups at different moments of the play just became a natural part of working on any script. I found myself going through the script with a kind of ceaseless dialogue in my head: *The female inmates will probably really laugh hard at this part; the men not so much. Homeless people might really connect with this character, especially if he is taken very seriously. I think this part of the play is really boring; I imagine that most audience members will think so, too. Nothing important is really happening here, so why don't I just cut it?* Being able to imagine a play through so many different lenses of experience has both multiplied and clarified the choices I can make as a director; it's now become a wonderful bubbling font of creative ideas.

ALL THE LIGHTS ON

BEING WRONG IS PART OF IT ALL   The other major danger of making assumptions about an audience is being wrong. And indeed, when you try to imagine through the eyes of others, you will very often be wrong. At Ten Thousand Things, we are so often wrong that we've come not only to accept error as necessary but to embrace it as a vital part of our work. Errors are just opportunities to learn and make discoveries. We like to make discoveries; we make a lot of them. The countless moments of being proven wrong in performance about the assumptions we've made could easily fill several volumes.

Our fourth tour, when we performed María Irene Fornés's *Mud* at our very first women's prison, I worried a lot about how the women would receive the ending, where the main character, Mae, who has been caring for her mentally impaired brother, Lloyd, is shot and killed by him. I worried that the women would see themselves in Mae, and the ending would be too tragic and sad to bear. But to our great surprise, after the gunshot, the women began to cry out, "Lloyd! Lloyd!" as, like a great child, he picked up his dead sister in his arms, not understanding at all what he had done. The women's sympathies instantly went to him. He was left alone, abandoned, without anyone to care for him. And there I learned the great lesson that for most women in prison, the constant black hole in their hearts is the children they have had to leave behind. Whenever a story offers the tiniest chance to release this anxiety, the women's emotions will instantly go there. They weren't that concerned with Mae's fate at all.

When we did *The Ballad of the Sad Cafe* (by Edward Albee, based on Carson McCullers's novella), I was certain that female inmates would love the main character, Miss Amelia, a tough loner in a small town in the south who wore overalls and ran the town's only general store. It turns out they did not like her very much at all. Their dislike intensified when, at a crucial moment, Miss Amelia wasn't able to make herself vulnerable. She was unable to receive a very sincere, heartfelt confession of love from Marvin Macy, an appealing ex-convict who was visiting town. Marvin got down on his knees and begged her to love him, but she said no. The women simply couldn't forgive such coldness. They gave the actress playing Miss Amelia very faint applause during the curtain call.

Another example of having our original assumption proved wrong occurred when we performed a new play based on ancient comic Kyogen tales, *At Your Service*, written for us by local storyteller Kevin Kling. Though double- and triple-casting was a hallmark of Ten Thousand Things performance style, I hadn't yet ventured into male gender-crossing, asking men to play women's parts, in part because I feel like men generally have enough good roles in theater as it is but also in part because I was more than a little worried how the male inmates might receive such casting. Days before rehearsal began, however, the only woman in this three-actor play had to drop out, and the only available actor with enough comic inventiveness to match hers was a man. He would have to play the female characters as well as some that could be either sex.

Necessity once again brought us to the brink. Setting up in the gym of the first men's prison of the tour, we were all more than a little terrified, fearing the men might start mocking the actor and the play. In my short introduction, I made it a point to say that a male actor would be playing the women's roles, just as was done in ancient Japan, when women were not allowed onstage. I noticed a shift in the men at that point; this seemed to make an impression

Bradley
Greenwald and
Jim Lichtscheidl,
At Your Service,
Hubbs Center
for Lifelong
Learning, 2005.

ALL THE LIGHTS ON

on them, appealing to their own sense of importance (though perhaps not for quite the right reasons—but we went with it). When the first female character appeared onstage, the men seemed very receptive, even approving, laughing heartily at the humor in the scene but not at all in a meanspirited way. Our assumptions had been misguided; our relief was profound.

THE LENS OF THE TRADITIONAL AUDIENCE   And now we can see that our paying audience is also just one small group, with its own specific experiences that cause it to behave and respond in certain fairly predictable ways. We can make assumptions about them based on our experiences with them, aware of their specificities because of our ability to compare them with other groups. They are generally much quieter. They don't laugh as much at bawdy humor. They notice different details of the play because of their educational backgrounds. It is sometimes challenging for the actors, who have become accustomed to liveliness and open honesty from our other audiences, to make the shift, but we have found aspects of the listening of our more financially comfortable audiences that we appreciate as well.

More important, our paying audiences can surprise us, too, breaking out of the mold. *The Seven*, a hip-hop retelling of Aeschylus's *The Seven Against Thebes*, by playwright Will Power, gave our expectations a delightful jolt. Our main anxiety in presenting this play, which tells the story of two brothers trying to overcome their father's curse and peacefully share power, lay with our traditional audiences' willingness to venture into this musical world fraught with the n-word and the f-bomb. And at the beginning of each paying show, I reminded people that we often ask our nontraditional audiences to step onto unfamiliar linguistic turf, as when we do Shakespeare or Beckett, but that this time, we were asking some of them to step into unfamiliar territory instead, and we hoped they would keep open minds and enjoy the ride. Though each audience seemed a bit taken aback in the opening minutes, it didn't take long for these generally over-sixty, predominantly upper-middle-class audiences to start to bop along with the actors, surprising us and often themselves, sometimes even raising their hands above their heads and swaying their arms to the music. Many approached us afterward to tell us how deeply the story had moved them—and how much they had enjoyed hip-hop. Paying audiences, too, love being surprised.

Imagining an audience means making assumptions about a group of people so that you can begin a conversation with them. What is crucial is that you become as aware as you possibly can of these assumptions and know that the audience will tell you when you are wrong. At Ten Thousand Things we now heartily, and with great pleasure, embrace the strong possibility that many of our assumptions *will* be wrong. Our mistakes, sometimes painful, sometimes delightful, are our opportunities. Holding them thus, lightly, in awareness lets us open ourselves in humility to keep making discoveries about the boundless capacities of human beings. This conversation seems a fine thing for theater to strive for.

In a strange way, this really is all just a way to make myself bigger. Like most directors, when I decide to work on a script, I start with me, with my own likes and dislikes of the material. Performing for so many different groups of people has given me an amazing opportunity to broaden and extend myself as I try to understand how others might see it, too. Such imagining has made me a bigger human being, and as a result, I firmly believe, a better artist. This simple act of trying to imagine how others experience the world is really the essence of theater. All actors, directors, designers, and playwrights try to do so through the eyes of different characters in a play. It's strange how rarely we try to do this through the eyes of our audience. But I think that's because our audiences are right now, for the most part, all the same. This is a sad, self-imposed poverty for the theater, especially as we grasp the overwhelming wealth of experience that truly varied and diverse audiences can bring to us as theater makers.

Bruce A. Young as Oedipus, *The Seven*, at Open Book, 2012.

ALL THE LIGHTS ON

Aimee K. Bryant, *Ragtime*, women's correctional facility, 2005.

3

FAIRY TALES—BIG ENOUGH STORIES
Choosing a Script

PEOPLE OFTEN ASK how I choose plays for Ten Thousand Things, and my first answer is that it's always been very intuitive. When reading scripts, I wait for a pull in my gut, one that alerts me not only that I am finding this play very interesting but that our diverse audiences probably will, too. That's it. That's how I choose. At first glance, the list of plays we've done over the years seems somewhat puzzling and random: *King Lear, The Unsinkable Molly Brown, The Ballad of the Sad Café, Antigone, Blood Wedding, Ragtime, Doubt, Endgame.* But stepping back, I can see that these plays all actually share a great deal in common and can better articulate what goes into causing me to feel that pull.

PLAYS FOR AUDIENCES WITH WEALTH From the treasure box of the lenses of different audience perspectives, I almost always started by choosing the lens that let me see a story through the eyes of those without wealth. Looking through this lens, I was astonished at how many plays in Western dramatic literature really seemed to be written for audiences with a good deal of money. So many plays from centuries past are about wealthy young couples foiled by their parents in attempts to marry their true loves. So many contemporary plays are about relationships or marriages of well-off couples gone sour or careers not going as planned. A friend once dubbed this category of contemporary drama, currently quite popular on Broadway and in the regional theater, "Rich People Being Mean to Each Other." The struggles of such stories felt small, at least when compared to the prospect of not being able to find food or shelter for your children, or not being able to find a job because you can't read, or being thrown into prison. I didn't think my nontraditional audiences would be that interested in these more cushioned "problems."

And yet my intuition also told me that contemporary, realistic plays about living in poverty could be disastrous. In the first place, our low-income audiences would know far more about those situations than we, as mostly middle-class artists, ever could. We could meet in a "make-believe" slum, as we had in *The Good Person*, but not in one realistically re-created around detailed knowledge of poverty today. It felt arrogant to think we would have anything to contribute: we would most likely appear ignorant and clumsy. To top it off, living in poverty was so often painful, why would anyone actually living in it want to experience more of it? It made me realize that many plays about contemporary poverty are probably written for wealthy audiences as well, to help them better understand existences different from their own. This is not a bad thing, but it's not what we were out to do here.

ONCE UPON A TIME   Looking at scripts from this vantage point helped to quickly eliminate a great many in my stack. I approached the remaining ones once again with my intuition; I began to see similarities in the ones that pulled at me. I like to call these types of plays "fairy tales." A fairy tale is a story that lets us all, no matter what our background or economic status, enter its world together as equals. Fairy tales are also, quite conveniently, the kinds of plays that I have always most enjoyed. They are the stories I actually think theater tells the best, better than any other art form.

First and foremost, fairy tales wrestle with very deep struggles, ones that every human being knows in the bones. Stories of the unrelenting hold of jealousy, the pain of great betrayal, the violent urge for revenge. They offer no easy answers, and thus are stories that respect their audiences, knowing that all of us have been wrestling with these huge issues for centuries, without much success. No one of us really knows, better than anyone else, how to answer the questions a fairy tale raises.

Setting has a great deal to do with the fairy tale's broad appeal. These are stories that happen in another time and another place, usually, though not always, outside the scope of actual human history, places and times where,

ALL THE LIGHTS ON

again, none of us can be expert. In our contemporary, realistic world, some of us are experts in the details of poverty; others are experts in the details of middle-class comfort or upscale wealth. But none of us really knows what it is to be a king or a queen. We all like to imagine ourselves as royalty, at the center of the world, as someone of supreme importance and worthy of being loved. But we all enter this terrain as novices. So through its setting, too, a fairy tale creates a level playing field on which we all are equals.

MULTIPLICITY OF CHARACTERS Because they are such big stories, fairy tales usually have lots of characters, from lots of different classes. Such teeming populations are hard to find in the economically restricted storytelling required of contemporary playwrights by so many theaters today, theaters worried about cast sizes and budgets. But having many different characters onstage provides access to many more different points of view. Because we have created a theater that performs for people of so many experiences, particularly economic ones, often seated together at the same performance, the ability to consider many points of view in one story is crucial.

In a fairy tale world, anyone can be anything. These nonrealistic worlds, unbound by the painful histories of oppression in our own, allow for creative and diverse casting. It's no problem to have Puerto Rican kings and African American queens with a Korean American son for the prince, alongside female warriors and jesters. There is room for anyone to be almost anything in a fairy tale world, and this allows us to extend the invitation to enter the story even more compellingly to all. And because so many of the places where we perform are not only very racially mixed but often racially charged and tense (as in many prisons), it has become important for us to create, for an hour or two anyway, a world where race doesn't matter so much. The relief of an audience, once they've realized that for a little while they can let down their guard about race, is palpable; entering such a fairy tale world becomes part of their ability to relax and enjoy.

PERSPECTIVE ON PAIN A fairy tale's far-away setting can provide imaginative distance from deep pain in a way that contemporary naturalistic plays cannot.

In our early days, we worked with a playwright who, though he tried to comply with my exhortations to set his story in a made-up place, ended up locating much of it in a very realistically detailed contemporary urban world. The story concerned a mother and a teenage daughter, both drug addicts, who each ended up losing her child to foster care. There is probably nothing more painful than losing a child. I remember a performance at a shelter where droves of women got up to leave in the middle of the play. The events were simply too painful to watch. Why would anyone who had experienced such a wrenching separation ever want to go through it again? Such a realistic story was not wanted or needed; it just hit too close to home. It was probably our hardest Ten Thousand Things tour ever. I vowed it would never happen again and have remained fiercely devoted to fairy tales ever since.

And indeed, through fairy tales we have been able to do plays about losing a child that people can bear. Brecht's *The Caucasian Chalk Circle* tells of a child, born of a wealthy woman but abandoned in war, found and cared for by a poor kitchen maid, whose true mother is uncertain. Near the play's end, the child is placed in a circle in a contest between the two women, the winner being the one who can pull hard enough to drag him out. Grusha, the adoptive mother, doesn't want to cause injury, so of course she lets go. She then has to watch her child walk away with someone else. Set in a made-up time and place, though, the pain of this sight was much easier for our audiences to watch; the fairy tale setting granted distance and perspective.

Of course Grusha gets her child back in the end. But even with the Greek tragedies which do not end so happily, like *Iphigenia*, where Clytemnestra's child is killed in a sacrifice to the gods, the loss is easier to watch because the story takes place so long ago and far away. There is comfort in knowing that you are not alone, that others before you have also suffered so unfairly. Because of imaginative distance, male and female inmates, all separated from their children, were able to sit and watch these plays straight through, gaining perspective on and solace for their own situations.

OPEN SPACE INVITES ACTIVE IMAGINATIONS   Fairy tales contain so many other enticements to audiences: most wonderfully, they ask everyone to jump in and use their imaginations full blast. Because no one can be an expert at what a fairy tale world is actually like, the stories contain lots of space for us to fill in, especially in a Ten Thousand Things performance situation where we have almost no set. A homeless woman can imagine what a palace looks like just as well as a suburban housewife. With fairy tales we need fewer "things" to help us imagine the world. Blenders and toasters and large-screen TVs placed on the stylish shelves of the elaborately reconstructed walls of a split-level suburban home can serve as a barrier to people who are constantly reminded, every time they look at the set, of what they do not have. But a sword or a scepter or a scroll, a simple strange object that almost no one these days actually possesses, can invite everyone to fill in the space around it.

Fairy tales free up all of us to concentrate on more important things than "the correctness of the objects." So often, when I go to realistic contemporary plays, I find myself thinking about whether the props or costumes are right, whether that kind of person would actually have that kind of armchair in their living room or that kind of can opener in their kitchen or wear that particular style of skirt or those particular shoes. Since no one can be an expert in a made-up world, we are all free to concentrate on other matters: whether emotional depths ring true, whether the behavior of the characters seems ethical or just. Fairy tales point our attentions more firmly toward the questions that unite us rather than the material things that so often divide and create hierarchy.

ROOM FOR MOVEMENT A fairy tale also invites lots of movement. You don't usually find sofas or armchairs there; fairy tales usually don't require large furniture pieces that encourage actors to sit down and talk and talk and create sinkholes of static energy onstage. The invented worlds of fairy tales are filled with so many more possibilities for movement: Characters can break the confines of the small gestures to which we usually limit ourselves in everyday life. People can skip and spin and leap. A sudden spurt across the stage, a sharp turn, or an abrupt halt, each draws our focus and helps to physicalize what is going on underneath all the words. If a play is set in another time and place but requires people just to sit and talk for lengthy periods, it probably is not the right play for the diversity of our audiences. Surprising physical movement helps so much to clarify and intensify the story.

The large, open spaces of fairy tales, I firmly believe, make them the kinds of stories that theater tells best. We can tell them far better than film or television. I so often wish that theaters would acknowledge this and stop trying to be like TV or movies. Neither of those dramatic storytelling mediums can have any empty space. The camera must record the reality in front of it, and this guarantees that all the backgrounds will be filled in: all the bricks in the wall, all the buildings along the street, all the trees on the mountains inescapably fill the frames. When a film tells a story about a world none of us knows, it still does all the imagining for us, filling in exactly what the boarding school for young wizards looks like or presenting a flying dragon in the flesh through special effects. Science fiction and fantasy worlds must be presented in full "realistic" detail. There is no empty space for our imaginations to participate in their creation, and as a result the worlds are flattened: the details are already complete.

ALL KINDS OF PLAYS QUALIFY   Of course all kinds of stories can be fairy tales—they don't have to take place in make-believe kingdoms with palaces. There are endless ways to create the imaginative distance of "fairy." A story set in an actual historical period, one different from our own, like the musical *Ragtime* or Strindberg's *Miss Julie*, can easily be interpreted as a fairy tale. Many in our audience have little knowledge of history anyway, so this frees us from having to worry about re-creating the actual historical world in accurate detail. Authentic period costumes like ruffs and stockings for Shakespeare or elaborate and accurately flounced and frilled gowns would most likely serve as a barrier to many nontraditional audiences, who immediately associate such trappings with "rich, white people stories" anyway, so a fairy tale perspective frees us from all that. Even a more contemporary story like John Patrick Shanley's *Doubt*, which tells of the struggle between a nun and a priest, can be seen from a fairy tale perspective. Though many in our audiences have had direct experience of being abused as a child or being falsely accused of a crime, the world of a 1960s Catholic monastery, with the strange robes and

caps of its inhabitants, was exotic enough to provide distance from the pain of the issues. It just has to be "another time, another place." We can invent the rest together.

But I have watched Ten Thousand Things audiences enough now to confidently assert that although there are many ways to bring make-believe distance onto the stage without having actual "fairies," there must be a *tale*. I myself am often attracted to nonlinear, experimental plays; I enjoy plunging in and trying to make my own sense of it all—but I have had practice and training over the years to help me become familiar and comfortable with such experiences. Many in our first-time theater audiences have not been afforded this luxury, and as a company we do not have time to educate. We come in to perform for what are often very transient populations, groups that fluctuate dramatically day to day. Story, however, is something we all can grasp right away. We need no explanation or education around it; every human has deep experience with it. Story is the thread that we all, across the entire spectrum of humanity, can hold onto, together; story will pull us all through from beginning to end.

A SCRAP OF HOPE, A LIGHT TO SHARE   There's one more requirement to choosing a story for Ten Thousand Things, however. From these many years of performing for people who have led very difficult lives, I've come to believe that, no matter how dark the telling, no matter how deep the probing of human misdeeds, the tales we choose to tell must contain a tiny shard of hope. We all need just a little something to seize onto, some tiny thread that allows us to keep moving forward a little, that allows for some possibility of change. I have come to feel morally responsible for finding this tiny shard in every story. If it's not apparent, I dig hard to find at least a bit of it. This has nothing to do with happy endings, of course, which we all know are impossibly rare. But even to have been able to perceive that for one character at one moment another choice was possible, even if that choice was not ultimately made—even just that can provide a scrap of hope.

I have come to see that choosing to tell a story without any hope, as sometimes happens in contemporary plays, is an indulgence. It feels to me, ironically, a possibility born of the luxury of having a comfortable cushion. Telling a story without hope is a *choice* artists make because none of us knows for sure whether there is or is not hope for humanity. I know that I need hope to function. These days, as temperatures on our planet continue to rise unabated, as the economic gap continues to widen, as our country is divided again and again along racial lines, I spend lots of time searching for hope myself. It's hard work. I want to come by any hope honestly, of course, by looking reality squarely in the face. But I still need to see things in such a way that I won't be paralyzed with despair. A scrap of hope allows us to try to change until the last possible moment. We have none of us reached that last moment, so I believe we must search hard to find a way to honestly tell our stories with hope. As artists now, I believe a big part of our job is to work mightily to find some bit of possible light to share.

ACCESS TO NAÏVETÉ   And then there is that word "fairy," which, in the way we use it, has almost nothing to do with actual fairies but a great deal to do with naïveté. Naïveté is another great leveler. It comes from the place of the child in each of us, the child who has participated in making things up and believing, at least for a while, that what she has created is real. Theater asks us, as adults, to behave naïvely in each other's presence: to believe that the aluminum pole is a tree, that the actor with long furry ears is a donkey, that the actress whose hands are covered with red dye has just murdered someone. Such full-throttle make-believe is not something most of us are comfortable doing publicly in our regular adult lives. But if the pull of the story is strong enough, we all end up doing it anyway.

And with Ten Thousand Things, the adults do it, not hidden in the dark, but in full fluorescent light, in a circle where everyone can be seen. The moment when everyone looks up at once to discover that we've all been engaged in this ridiculous activity together is a wonderful equalizer. With so little on-stage, it's very clear that the world is only held together by our pretending. We share a moment of embarrassed laughter. And we are reminded in a funny way that we were all once children. This moment is a crucial equalizer, and I always try to make sure that the first such moment happens fairly early on in the show. We acknowledge the ridiculousness of it all together, and then we can all jump back into the story and get on with it.

And thus, the heightened naïveté required by a fairy tale also guarantees that the audience will always be able to find laughter. In fairy tale worlds it's so much easier to step back and see that we're just making it all up. This is critical in the challenging worlds that these stories so often explore. Laughter is absolutely necessary to survive darkness onstage or off. It's actually profoundly important practice for people who are afforded little occasion to laugh in their daily lives. Indeed, the act of laughter almost always offers its own shard of hope. The darker the world, the more vital flashes of humor become to allow us to truly see in the darkness.

It is often challenging to find contemporary plays that are written with these kinds of attributes. That's why I was extremely lucky to discover, living just twelve blocks away from me in Minneapolis, a fantastic playwright, Kira

Obolensky, who writes naturally from the perspective of "fairy tales." Kira loves to create, with great humor, worlds that are different from the ones we inhabit in our everyday lives; her language is simple but playful and heightened just enough to lift us out of our own time and place. Because she lives so close by, she's been able, over the years, to attend performances for almost every kind of audience group, and she now carries these audiences around in her head as she writes. When writers start to imagine what stories they would choose to tell if they knew that the true diversity of humanity would be sitting in their audience and not just the small homogenous sliver they are most familiar with, their stories just naturally start to expand. Kira has been surprised and delighted to discover what has happened to her writing as she has continued to do such imagining of the audience. It is exciting to think what might happen to the American theater if more playwrights could similarly experience and began to write for audiences containing many classes, cultures, and lives outside the "traditional" spectrum.

It's important to note that all these "guidelines" for choosing a play should be broken if your intuition tells you a different kind of story might connect. Many wonderful guest directors have proposed plays that at first seemed to me to fall outside my experience of what would engage our hugely diverse populations. When Peter Rothstein wanted to do *Doubt* or Lear de Bessonet proposed *Streetcar*, I worried the stories might be too contemporary and realistic, too narrow in scope, or without enough distance from pain. I was delighted to have my fears allayed. Both directors understood the strangeness of the plays' worlds and the deep universal resonance of the stories. Each one actually found the "fairy tale" in plays that at first glance seemed too small and specific. I was delighted to see how well each of these seemingly unlikely plays could work.

And it could very well be that a group of actors and a director with great understanding and experience of the contemporary world of poverty could do a realistic story about the here and now with great success. Part of my reluctance to do so certainly has to do with my relative ignorance about such lives and is an honest acknowledgment of my own limitations and those of most of the actors I work with, though part of it also has to do with my strong sense

ALL THE LIGHTS ON

that these realistic plays do not provide enough imaginative distance from pain. But I certainly could be wrong.

I do believe, however, that "fairy tales" are still the best meeting place for *all* of us, allowing theater to work full force and generating maximum radiance. Their wide-open spaces contain enough room to invite in every kind of human to use their imaginations full throttle, to become naïve and to pretend, with easy access to humor, to laugh at the ridiculousness of it all. Because there's so little clutter, it's easier to see connections between things. Against an empty backdrop, each object, each person, each situation becomes more heightened and resonant. Our imaginations have room to caress what is there and can more easily spot connections and metaphors. Fairy tales combined with the empty spaces of theater allow us the room to more easily find food for our souls, which are always searching for meaning and connection with each other. For the wide diversity of our audiences, they are truly, I believe, the stories that theater is best suited to tell.

Karen Wiese-Thompson as a ghost and Kris Nelson as Raskolnikov in Kira Obolensky's *Raskol*, House of Charity, 2009.

Greta Oglesby as Clytemnestra in *The Furies*, Dorothy Day Center, 2001.

4

AUDIENCES AT LIFE'S EXTREMES—THE GREEKS
Fairy Tale Group #1

MY ONLY EXPERIENCE watching Greek tragedies before Ten Thousand Things came in my early twenties. I'd be seated in a large theater, usually toward the back, a long distance from the actors who were emoting full force onstage. I was working nine-to-five temp jobs, and like many people around me, I was tired from the day, struggling to keep my eyes open and to find a way to connect to people who were murdering their family members or suffering from enormous loss of loved ones who'd been killed. (In fact, one of my all-time favorite audience comments came from a women's prison where we were doing *Iphigenia*. An inmate sitting down before the show picked up the program we had placed on her chair and declared, "I don't wanna see no damn Greek pathology!")

Despite these experiences, after the first *Good Person* tour, while I was casting my nets far and wide to find the next play, my intuition drew me to Greek tragedies. I paged through stories from long ago, brutal worlds of kings and queens and their offspring. The plays addressed huge questions that humans haven't stopped struggling with, so often centering on our almost compulsive need for vengeance. The struggle between the pain of being wronged and the need to ease that pain by doing wrong in return seems one of the most eternal of all. All signs pointed to a "fairy tale," a big story in another time and place that might somehow connect with its exploration of enormous life struggles.

At the same time, I dreamed about other places we might go to find first-time audiences. I kept returning to one experience on the *Good Person* tour where we'd performed at a shelter just for women. The freedom and emotional responsiveness of that particular audience remained with me. That site had provided our biggest burst of radiance, and it seemed promising territory to continue to explore. How often do we get to perform for audiences of only women? Such audiences would have a hunger for complex, intelligent, and powerful female characters that matched my own. All of this was swirling around inside me when I stopped at *Electra* by Sophocles. Once again matching an audience somewhat simply and obviously to the play's main character, I tried to think of where we might find young women, like Electra, who were familiar with painful cycles of betrayal and revenge. I decided we would try to perform this tragedy for girls in detention.

ELECTRA: THE PRIMAL URGE FOR VENGEANCE The events of the play felt suddenly relevant to me as I knew that many juveniles in prison have been "betrayed" by their families: abused physically or emotionally, neglected, or abandoned. I thought at least the rough contours of the situation would resonate. At the beginning of the story, Electra's mother has murdered her father. Agamemnon had just returned from battle and was cleaning his wounds in the bath when Clytemnestra stabbed him with a knife, in vengeance for his murder of their older daughter; he'd sacrificed Iphigenia's blood to the gods so he could win the war. But Clytemnestra's motives don't concern Electra. All she knows is that she deeply loved her father and her mother has betrayed her. Electra is consumed with hatred, finding herself a servant in her own home, ignored and dismissed by her mother and a new stepfather.

In my rough imaginings, one particular line of Electra's leapt out: "Hope is dying inside me. With evil all around me, how can I keep myself sane and whole and moderate?" It seemed that question might really resonate with a young woman finding herself alone in prison.

This Greek "fairy tale" offered no easy answers. The tension of *Electra* comes from not being able to say whether she is a victim of the vicious cycle of her family's violence or whether she is evil and out of control for helping her brother murder their mother. Of course I did not want to present Electra as just a victim, nor did I want to view the audience simply as victims. I imagined that at least some of the young women found themselves in prison for truly doing wrong, no matter how badly they themselves had been treated. The complicated reality of my imagined audience again urged me to look at the complexity of the story; it made me want to heighten the play's tensions and hard edges, giving all sides a fair hearing, all characters their due. The Chorus, with their periodic questions and responses, seemed like an excellent vehicle to help the audience process this complexity. Most important, the play ended with a big question, just as *The Good Person* had, with the Chorus asking the audience, "What shall we say of this? Are we free from Evil? Or caught in more Evil? What is Good and Evil? I do not know."

I knew that girls of all racial backgrounds would be in the audience, and the story's fairy tale setting allowed me space to create a world where anyone could be anything. I was able to cast a wide array of excellent, racially diverse actors, something easy to do in Los Angeles. In such a made-up world, a Puerto Rican queen could be mother to a white daughter, a Chicana daughter, and an African American son. In addition to offering the pleasure of being able to see oneself onstage, such casting felt healing somehow. If race didn't matter to the family, it probably wouldn't have to matter so much to the audience, either. I imagined that prisons could be very racially charged situations, and such families might allow the audience to brush racial politics aside at least for a while, almost in relief. At one level, I hoped, this casting might confirm our deepest instincts that such "fairy tale families" should really be possible.

We did only three performances of the play. It was all still so new, and I wanted to be sure to pay people fairly this time. Since *The Good Person*, I had figured out how to become a nonprofit using some DIY software and had managed to obtain a small grant for the project from the city of Los Angeles.

Our most powerful performance took place in an LA County juvenile prison. It was a shockingly grim place where both young women and men were sent. The old brick buildings were gloomy and foreboding. My heart skipped several beats as we walked past rows of young men in bright orange jumpsuits lined up in a courtyard, hands clasped behind their backs, a few at the ends of the lines so small that they couldn't have been older than ten or twelve.

There were two dingy common rooms for the girls, one with cafeteria tables and Saturday-morning cartoons blaring from television sets suspended from the ceiling, the other, our performance space, a small room of gray cinderblock with several wide steplike ledges on three sides on which the girls could sit, dim light filtering through grated windows. A few girls elected to stay in the other room and watch cartoons, but most, probably about thirty, decided to see what we were up to. Two girls in their mid-teens sat on the top ledge, both of them sucking their thumbs, making it clear that many here were really, at bottom, in need of comfort. Who could imagine they might find it in a Greek tragedy?

As the musician began to drum, this small group of young women entered the turbulent world of the House of Agamemnon effortlessly. Although the actors were plumbing deep, complex emotions just inches away, the girls were at ease with the intensity; it seemed these extremes were comfortable and familiar. There was no need for them to strain to connect. They absorbed it all: Electra's enormous outpourings of grief at her father's murder, her arguments with her quieter and more pragmatic sister, her ragings at her mother, her joy at the return of her long-absent brother Orestes. They sat intently as the plot unfolded and followed with acceptance and ease each twist and turn, from Electra's successful enlistment of her brother in the plan to kill their mother to her deep satisfaction as her stepfather unrolled the sheets to discover Clytemnestra's corpse. The sudden shifting extremes of Greek tragedy seemed a familiar reflection of the emotional roller coasters of their own adolescent lives. They sat quite still, taking it all in. I felt again that the distance of this long-ago "fairy tale" world made their ease possible in a way a contemporary retelling would not allow.

Once the story was done, they eagerly broke their silence. Without any prompting from us, they began to ask questions. It was the most seamless transition from play to discussion I have ever witnessed. "Did they kill people like that in the old days?" one voice asked. "Is this a true story?" "It's a myth," an actress replied. "It represents feelings we all have inside us. All of us have the potential to love, to hate, to want revenge, to kill, don't you think?" The girls nodded their assent. "How does it feel to act out murdering people?" one girl asked Orestes. "I'm still not sure I really know," replied the actor quite honestly. "I know how it feels to *want* to kill someone."

ALL THE LIGHTS ON

Then a quiet voice spoke from the top ledge: "My mother killed my father, so I know how Electra feels. It stays with you always." All of us onstage took deep breaths, letting the reality of this statement sink in. We felt the shock of realizing that we were not just telling a story or a myth; we were treading very real and difficult paths that many in our audience knew only too well. As artists we could never let ourselves pretend we really understood those paths; we could only keep searching for a deeper understanding. Once again we were overwhelmed with a profound sense of humility. In case any of us had forgotten, we were reminded that this state of mind was absolutely necessary for our own artistic work.

The girls spoke to the *characters* more often than the actors. "How does it feel to be a servant in your own mother's house?" they asked Electra. "How could you treat your own daughter like a servant?" they demanded of Clytemnestra. She replied, "Electra reminds me of my husband, who killed my daughter Iphigenia. Every time I look at her, I'm reminded of this man I hate. So I don't mind having her out of my sight. And I'm under the influence of my new husband." Aegisthus, Clytemnestra's lover, chimed in, "Doesn't bother me at all. Electra could live in a pigsty for all I care." The girls hooted.

Next came a debate about whether it was better to be outspoken and brash, like Electra, or more quiet and politic like her sister Chrysothemis. "Chrysothemis was a hypocrite!" cried one girl. "No, no way, Electra was an asshole!" averred another. The actress playing Chrysothemis chimed in, "From my point of view, Electra's ranting and raving weren't doing any good. She was still weak, even though she acted so tough." "Yes, yes!" agreed about half of the girls.

The young women identified keenly with the arguments between Electra and her mother. "I was crying, you reminded me of my mother so much!" one girl explained. The actress playing Clytemnestra later confided that whenever she spoke to Electra, she had only to speak, in her mind, to the girls in the audience, and her heart instantly opened and was torn in two, as was Clytemnestra's. The audience, once again, made our artistry better.

All in the audience could clearly see the cycle of violence and revenge in this ancient tale, easily connecting it to forces at play in their own communities. They saw the stupidity of the murders and yet seemed to understand how easily one can be swept up into the machinations of that very powerful urge for vengeance. There was even sympathy for the callous stepfather Aegisthus, who, when faced with his own death by Orestes's hand, had cried out,

Wait. Think. Both of you.

How will it end?

I helped kill your father.

You helped your brother to kill me.

So someone of my kin

Will have to kill you both

And it will go on forever.

Our house is accursed.

So . . . what will you do?

Go on doing Evil

and saying you do Justice?

What does that gain? Tell me.

At that moment, most of the girls were on his side.

The girls were interested in the extreme racial mix of the family and expressed their appreciation of it. Not only did this confirm my instincts that diverse racial casting around family groupings could actually help to set aside race as an issue, allowing everyone to move more quickly into the story, but I discovered that for many, such a family makeup was not a "fairy tale." Some of the girls offered that they actually came from such racially diverse families themselves. It was gratifying for them to see the reality of their families—often composed of stepparents and stepsiblings of different races, families breaking apart and reassembling—reflected onstage.

I was happy when one girl asked, "Why did you decide to do this play for us?" This is always a key question for an audience to whom we bring a play, rightly suspicious of strangers and their "do-gooder" motives. Though I always try to make very clear that we are not preaching in the presentation of the actual play itself, I was glad to have a chance to answer the question directly and emphasize that we were not passing judgment on any characters.

"We wanted to explore feelings of revenge, which we all have," I said, "and to look at what happens when you act on them." The actress playing Clytemnestra added, "And to see whether, if you can see the history, the cycle, the pattern, then perhaps you can find a way to break out of it." The girls murmured in understanding.

They offered up unsolicited praise: "It took lots of guts to concentrate like that with all of us in front of you." The fundamentals of theater, which we completely took for granted, were wondrously strange to them. "I like how you guys were really serious and it's like the seven of you didn't even realize we were right in front of you." Perhaps most gratifying of all was the comment, "I really appreciate you taking this really old play and finding things in it that have to do with what's going down now." Once again, we received confirmation of our intuition that the imaginative distance of a story set in "another time, another place" would actually allow deep connections to occur.

As we carried our set pieces back to our cars that afternoon, we felt elated. We were all moved by how the girls had taken things so personally, causing us once again to wonder at how rarely paying audiences allow themselves to admit that they have been personally affected by what they see onstage, how rarely they talk about a *play's* speaking directly to their own lives. The actor playing Orestes, carrying a drum and keyboards, turned to me to ask, "Is that what you had in mind?" Oh, yes, and ever so much more. By taking a big story of theater to people who had never seen it before, we had uncovered radiance: moments where the audience's response to the play was intense, profound, and even transcendent.

INSURMOUNTABLE OBSTACLES: PERFORMANCE CONDITIONS Every Ten Thousand Things "tour" is an unpredictable adventure, and although the *Electra* tour was short, in addition to this exhilarating performance, in keeping with the emotional roller coaster of Greek tragedy, we also experienced our first excruciating show, one where we could make almost no connection with the audience at all. And though at the time we were quite shaken, in hindsight I now can clearly see that it was the conditions of the performance that made it all so awful, rather than the actual performance itself.

I had heard that there was going to be a conference of Chicano youth at risk around the same time as our tour. That seemed a promising audience, so I contacted staff at the hosting organization and they were willing to try a performance. But when we arrived at the meeting space, we found ourselves carrying our urns and painted flats into a cavernous gymnasium. Assembled within was a teenage audience of both sexes. A mixture which, we quickly discovered, unleashes its own large and very different dynamic: the presence of the boys seemed to cause the girls to become quiet and subdued. In addition, the teens had been required by adults to attend as part of the conference. This created a hostile barrier that I have since learned is almost always impenetrable. All the lights in the gym were turned off and we were lit with a few very bright spotlights so that we could not see the audience at all, except for a few scowling faces in the very front row. It was quite clear no one wanted to be there, and we weren't able to draw them in—the barriers of darkness and mixed-sex teenagers not present by their own choice were just too much. We left feeling defeated. And yet, as has happened on every tour since, we clung tightly to our exhilarating experience at the girls' correctional facility. When the performance conditions had been right, the play really had connected.

THE FURIES: **AN ENDING REVISIONED**   We've returned to the well of the Greeks many times since. And it's no accident that the stories work. Scholars seem to have reached a general consensus that audiences for Greek tragedies were huge, perhaps in the tens of thousands, and contained citizens of almost all classes, including prisoners who were released for the performance. This broad swath of humanity in the audience probably goes a long way to explain why the Greek playwrights work so well for Ten Thousand Things. But it is very important to note that while the Greek tragedies feature a host of complex and powerful female roles, Greek audiences included very few women. The plays themselves often reflect this misogynistic view. As is true of most of the theatrical canon, my creativity is called upon again by necessity because I am a woman presenting plays to audiences who are sometimes composed entirely of women. I have to make adjustments either in casting or in editing and interpretation to be certain that truly everyone is welcomed into the world of the play.

Ron Menzel as Orestes fleeing outside the audience circle, *The Furies*, Dorothy Day Center, 2001.

Years later, poring through the plays, I was especially attracted to *The Eumenides*, once again because of its prominent female characters, the dark and mysterious Furies. The play grapples with fundamental issues of justice, venturing beyond the personal world of *Electra*, taking family struggles into the bigger political world of government systems—and the gods. But reading the play with contemporary eyes—my own and those of my all-female audiences especially—the gulf between the play's original world view, in which the female characters are treated with contempt, and our own, seemed almost unfathomable.

The story of *The Eumenides* picks up where *Electra* leaves off, following Orestes after he has killed his mother and stepfather. I imagined lots of places where the story might resonate with our now very diverse nontraditional audiences. I thought many could identify with Orestes, fleeing to escape the wrath of the Furies, who want vengeance for his murder of Clytemnestra. I thought many might understand what it's like to run from feelings of guilt and blame and self-hatred for wrongdoings. I imagined many, particularly in our all-female audiences, might also identify with the rage of the Furies over a mother who was murdered by her own son. Indeed, I imagined that many could identify with both Orestes and the Furies and their need to throw themselves down to beg for mercy, whether of the court or of the gods. I imagined that the need to find some kind of relief from overwhelming, devouring feelings of vengeance or guilty torment would resonate; I felt most could connect with the deep desire to receive, through a judge's decree, at least some restoration of sanity.

The part of the play that most deeply concerned me was its "happy ending." Against all reason, Athena and the gods decide to rule in favor of Orestes, finding him innocent of the murder of his mother. Athena breaks a tie in the jury and casts the deciding vote for Orestes, using "the prerogative of the male" as her justification. In essence she rules in favor of Orestes because men are more important. Realizing that the Furies might be more than a little disturbed by this, she acts quickly to appease their wrath, promising them a "partnership" in ruling the city if only they will retreat into their cave. Within minutes, the Furies begin to sing praises of the goddess and her wisdom and fairness, blessing Thebes and retreating happily into their cave, their names being changed to the Eumenides, or the Benevolent Ones.

That this is considered a plausible ending, let alone a happy one, seems inconceivable, especially with such a judgment coming from a female goddess! Thinking of all the women in our audiences struggling with their own sense of self-worth, the contempt with which the Furies and Clytemnestra's ghost are treated was problematic, to say the least.

But I was drawn to the darkness of the injustice and decided to embrace all these "problems," those places where I did not respond at all favorably to what the play seemed to be saying, as an excellent opportunity to explore a

ALL THE LIGHTS ON

fundamental question, "How does one conduct one's life in the face of injustice?" I knew this was a challenge faced by many in our audience, who had often been the recipients of life's harshest injustices in many ways. Is there a way to live with dignity despite deep unfairness, without shutting down one's gifts and powers but instead using them, along with anger, to be a creative force for change? I really wanted to see if indeed there were any possible truthful way the Furies could transform so quickly into the Eumenides, knowing that so many in our audiences were also asked to quickly and cheerfully accept their unjust fates.

Because the scales were tipped *so* strongly in favor of the men, I began to consider ways I might reshape the play, to make it palatable for anyone today to watch. I tried to preserve as much of the original text as possible, as always looking for the simplest and sparest translation, but made several choice cuts where the misogyny was almost unbearable. I then enlisted the services of playwright Lisa D'Amour to help craft new language for the play's introduction. The original play leaves out the reason for Clytemnestra's murder of her husband—he did, after all, kill their child! We wanted the audience to understand that Clytemnestra's ghost, who appears in the play to urge the Furies on, has reason for her anger, that she was not just "another crazy woman." I wanted to be sure the complexity of the characters and situations was clear, something with which many other Greek tragedies were successful.

Then the world entered into our storytelling in a way we could not have anticipated. We began rehearsals just a few days after 9/11; Lisa had been in New York City on the day of the attack and had looked up at the giant smoking towers. Suddenly, the Furies and the urgency and difficulty of calming the forces of vengeance became very real, and we found ourselves slightly more sympathetic to Athena's plight. The unjust decision of the 2000 elections, with a tie in the electoral vote and the Supreme Court ruling that tipped the scales, was also quite present in our minds. (Though I cannot count on our nontraditional audiences to have detailed knowledge of politics, I ventured that this would be one story everyone knew.) I decided to invite them into the play a little more strongly than usual, offering them an opportunity to participate in the wielding of justice. Athena would choose a jury by offering twelve audience members a gold scarf to hang around their necks. This jury would decide whether Orestes or Clytemnestra and the Furies would win the trial. We didn't ask anyone to get out of their seats, understanding that too much audience participation can be uncomfortable. Athena's assistant handed each a cardboard ballot from which the juror could punch out a square for Orestes or Clytemnestra—complete with hanging chad. Then, of course, no matter what the actual audience vote was, Athena would always rule in favor of Orestes. We created our own rigged election, our own rigged system of justice, and audience members took great delight in seeing the connection with our current world. (We were fascinated to see how the actual punch card ballots were usually fairly evenly divided between the Furies and Orestes, no matter what kind of audience.)

As I explored the difficult ending of the play—the instant transformation of the Furies into the Eumenides—I decided I wanted to open up ways for them to express their wrath when first presented with Athena's decision. Imagining that our all-male audiences in prisons might be more dismissive of the Furies if they were only females, I cast a man as well as three women in the roles. In rehearsals I challenged them all to find the fastest way they could accept the incredibly unjust ruling, asking them to manage to say at least a few of the lines of blessing given by the Furies at the play's end. But the emotions at this juncture were so intense that many could not even form words. I thought that music might help; we turned to shape note singing as a way to invoke sounds to help with some kind of transformation. It was incredibly painful. Only one or two actors could get to the point of saying words. One was finally able to say the first part of one line, "Let no wind blow to tear the trees," while another repeated the end, "Singing for some, for others a life of tears." The others just made sounds. They all ended in silence, glowering.

The transformation of the Furies into the Eumenides remained incomplete at best. Watching the ending, one felt that it would take years before any of them got to any place of acceptance. The play became a powerful portrait of the embers of rage and pain that remain when injustice is thrust upon people. Many in our audiences watched the ending in tears. The feelings of being forced to live with enormous injustice were extremely familiar, though our nontraditional audiences usually related them to their own personal experiences within the criminal justice or social service systems, while our paying audiences tended to connect them to their pain over the politics of the recent presidential election.

ANTIGONE: IN THE BUSH YEARS   Each time we return to the Greeks, our audiences continue to shed light on the plays and help us discover new ways to perform them. During the Bush years, I was attracted to the play *Antigone*, with its exploration of righteousness and stubbornness and the problems these attitudes can create for humans. I invited playwright Emily Mann, who had been interested in our work, to adapt this story, both of us aware of how righteousness seemed to be strangling our very democracy. But as with any attempt to raise our audience's eyes to consider the larger political world, we had to start from what is very personal, which the Greeks do so well. I imagined that stubbornness and self-righteousness had gotten many in our audience into difficult situations in their lives and felt Antigone's story would resonate on a personal level with them as well.

Bob Davis as Creon, *Antigone*, Cornerstone Women's Shelter, 2005.

Antigone has a Chorus, usually a challenge because a group of people speaking the same thing at the same time seems extremely stiff and unnatural. But when we came to consider what this might be, in light of what audiences had taught us over the years, it did not seem a problem at all. Our audiences, who do not sit quietly and politely in the dark but who instead often comment continuously on the action of the play, judging the characters and situations, inspired us to see the Chorus in a completely new light. We decided to seat the members of the Chorus in the circle of the audience as well. The actors got up from their chairs to play certain characters when the story required and then sat back down when they were "offstage," becoming chorus members, always participating in the storytelling, commenting on what they saw. This further encouraged our audience to make their comments known, and *Antigone* became a livelier event (though I do not recall that we were successful in getting any of our paying audiences to make vocal comments; traditional theater audiences have been too well trained to follow the rules of theatergoing).

After one performance at a women's prison, Kate Eifrig, a tall and powerful white actress who played the fierce Antigone (matched in our production by the equally fierce Ismene, played with passionate intensity by the petite African American actress Sonja Parks), encountered two inmates, a large, gregarious white woman and her petite and quiet African American companion. The large woman asked if Kate had heard about a recent shooting in North Minneapolis. "Because that was her brother who was shot," she continued, looking at her quiet friend. "And she's worried right now that she won't be given a leave for her brother's funeral. So we were kind of nervous when we heard in the introduction what this play was about." She paused again to look at her friend and then continued, "But it was a real good story. You guys did a really good job. We're glad we came after all." The small black woman remained quiet. We were never really quite sure what she made of the experience. We can only hope that she found some comfort in knowing that she was not alone in her sufferings. But her silence served as a reminder of how fine a line we sometimes walk when we do plays about life's extremes for people who often experience those extremes in their daily lives. Most of the time, the imaginative distance of the stories seems to make it approachable. But that

ALL THE LIGHTS ON

distance is vital, and even with it we sometimes are unsure about our impact on individual audience members, as is true of all theater, I suppose.

The Greeks, writing plays more than two thousand years ago, have provided a powerful stream of fairy tales for the diverse audiences of Ten Thousand Things. Our audiences, in turn, have helped us to breathe new life into these very old stories, whether by helping us to better plumb at the depths of the characters' emotions, or inspiring us to reimagine the Chorus, or compelling us to make room for women's experiences of the world. I needed to find more such stories, with breadth and depth and power and imaginative distance. They were hard to find. Out of desperation, almost—out of necessity, certainly—I turned my gaze to a world I had never approached as a director before: the seemingly formidable works of a certain British playwright in the time of the first Queen Elizabeth.

Kate Eifrig as Antigone and Sonja Parks as Ismene, *Antigone*, Cornerstone Women's Shelter, 2005.

Suzanne Warmanen as the Duke and Sonja Parks as Isabella, *Measure for Measure*, Project Success, 2012.

5

"JUST TELL THE STORY"—SHAKESPEARE
Fairy Tale Group #2

A FEW YEARS INTO my casting about for big enough stories, I stumbled upon a highly intriguing one that wrestled with that very big question of what makes for good justice. In it, a duke puts one of his deputies in charge and goes into hiding so he can spy on what happens to the realm's justice system in his absence (or as a homeless man would later so aptly describe it, "It's like an episode of that TV show *Undercover Boss*"). The deputy unleashes a fierce moral righteousness: he immediately dusts off some old laws that call for anyone who has sex out of wedlock to be executed. The story takes us to the courts, to the streets, and into prison, with a huge swath of characters from all classes—prostitutes and barkeeps, legal professionals, religious clergy, and fallen nobility—all wrestling with the question of what is good justice or, even more precisely, what is it like to both judge others and be judged. The play was funny and dark, looking at sex and morality and hypocrisy, and presented no easy answers to the questions it raised. I felt like our audiences would love it. The only problem was—I had never directed Shakespeare before.

I was intimidated, to say the least. Somewhere in my education I had picked up the message that Shakespeare should only be directed by experts, those who had studied him in graduate school, who understood all the historical background and scholarly controversies as well as all the intricacies of meter and scansion. There was an aura of mystery and erudition around Shakespeare, and I had never even directed a scene from one of his plays. I felt unworthy of the task.

***MEASURE FOR MEASURE*: CLEAR, URGENT, LIVELY**   I began with the simple aware-ness of something that turned out to be very complicated—I would just have to make the story of *Measure for Measure* very clear. My limited experiences of watching Shakespeare were ones of straining to piece together what was happening onstage. I couldn't actually understand much of what people were saying, though they might be speaking in beautiful, rotund, oratorical tones. *Measure for Measure* had a complicated plot, not to mention elevated lan-guage. I was terrified that I might not be able to do it.

As part of my strong commitment to avoid condescension, the thought of altering the language never crossed my mind. I was fairly certain that if the story were clear, audiences would love its music and playfulness and power. I also wanted to keep the entire story, every twist and turn of the plot, intact while being aware that I myself would have a difficult time sitting through anything much longer than two hours. In addition, I knew that the necessary strictures of prison schedules, with periodic counts of inmates throughout the day, wouldn't allow for a longer show. It did seem like there was a lot of repeti-tion that could be cut. Sometimes characters would try to explain a metaphor they were using with a complex analogy that only made it more difficult to un-derstand what they were saying. If I cut that extra explanation, suddenly the original, simple metaphor sprang much more clearly into focus, and we could actually better digest and enjoy it. There were also cuts that would help shed the play of archaic phrases that I felt any audience, no matter their economic status or educational background, would be grateful not to have to spend time trying to decipher. I would also try to find ways to replace a necessary but ar-chaic word with a clearer one.

I knew I would have to work with the actors to make the stakes for each character *very* high so that the story had a fierce urgency and momentum. I knew that, as with all the other shows I'd done thus far, I would have to work to make every single moment lively and engaging so no one would ever be able to sit back in their chair and space out. Clear, urgent, lively. Other than that— I really didn't know. While that sense of not knowing felt pretty terrifying at first, I've since come to understand that coming from a place of *not* knowing, rather than expertise, is a very good way to approach Shakespeare's work.

I took heart from a line I found in the writings of the well-known British Shakespearean director Declan Donnelan: "The most important thing to remember about Shakespeare is that he's dead—and we're alive. It is an odd thing to perform a play that is 400 years old." We fondly remember these words at the start of rehearsal for every Shakespeare play.

ROOM FOR WOMEN   I began, as I do with all the plays I direct, with my own responses to the script. And again, as with almost any classic drama, I didn't like the amount of space I found for myself as a woman in *Measure for Measure*. The few female characters included a nun, a prostitute, and Julietta, a fallen young noblewoman with about three lines (she's fallen into disgrace because she is pregnant and unmarried). There was one other small, troubling role: Mariana, a rejected woman, living in isolation and in constant mourning for a man who had treated her badly, appearing briefly in only a few scenes near the end of the play. Women needed more space; my all-female prison audiences only added reinforcement to my own desires.

I determined that more of the characters needed to be women. I noticed it would actually be quite easy to cast a woman as the Duke. Her trusted advisor, Escalus, could be a woman, too. Rather than cast the usual elderly man in that role, a younger woman, smart and wise and more than a little ambitious, anxious to win her mentor's favor and climb up the ladder, would be a much more fun and interesting Escalus. This would give excellent actresses a chance to explore the wonderful complexities of these parts. Even more important, it would help open up the play to our own times, when women actually sometimes do get to be in charge. It would give all our audiences a chance to experience more aspects of the play from a fresher, female point of view.

Such casting would also help to alleviate the extremely disturbing experience I had when reading the play's ending. The Duke, who has disguised himself as a friar, returns to interfere in his underlings' bad decisions, throwing off his monk's robes and revealing himself to everyone in a dramatic coup. As part of it all, he proposes marriage to Isabella, the young nun-to-be. Throughout the play he has spied on Isabella; he has manipulated and deceived her into believing her brother has been killed. The play's "happy ending" with his marriage proposal to a woman he has greatly abused felt very disturbing to me. Keeping the women's prison audiences very close to my heart, I did not want the play to end with the prospect of such a troubling relationship, in which a woman puts aside all her questions and qualms about a man, as well as her religious convictions, and agrees to marriage. A female Duke, however, could open up new possibilities when she, at the end of the play, says simply, "Dear Isabella, I have a motion much imports your good, whereto if you'll a willing ear incline, what's mine is yours and what's yours is mine." Isabella is given no words to respond. The Duke just keeps talking, urging everyone quickly into the palace, assuring them all their questions will be answered.

A female Duke wouldn't need to be making a marriage proposal. If she just extended her gavel, we could think she was offering Isabella a partnership administering justice in the realm, having been much impressed with the young woman's ability to fight for her convictions as well as her astonishing ability to be merciful and forgive. Isabella's mind could still be full of lots of questions—as would our minds, too—but at least one of the questions wouldn't have to be about a marriage proposal from a somewhat creepy old man. I was quite weary of those scenarios, and I felt certain most women—in *all* our audiences—would likely be tired of them, too. I am always looking for ways to tell a different story than "Look! Men oppress women!" That story is all too familiar.

A NEW LENS   Having the main character now be a woman, I looked at the play differently. I noticed a very short scene at the top of Act IV, one that is usually cut because it involves a child. This child sings for a moment and then leaves; his relationship to anyone else in the play is never explained. He sings to Mariana, the jilted woman, who also has appeared suddenly very late in the story. Since the Child doesn't seem to add anything to the plot, I might have cut him, too—except that I was now seeing the play through a woman's eyes.

I started to pay attention to all the references to pregnancy and children in the play, as well as all the times characters use wombs and full bellies as metaphors. Julietta, the fallen noble woman with only a few lines, is paraded through town with her large belly (silently, of course). We also learn peripherally that Lucio, a street character, has fathered a child with a prostitute, Kate

Keepdown, who is herself unseen in the play. Children without fathers are a result of having sex out of wedlock. The play is filled with references to punishing people for having sex without being married, which seems ridiculous to us, of course. But when you look through the eyes of female characters, it's easy to see that such profligate behavior does have troubling consequences: it lets fathers off the hook, especially for assuming their fair share of responsibility for their child's upbringing, financial and otherwise. A female Duke might be very interested in this problem, as might many of the single mothers in our audience. Suddenly, an issue we might be dismissive of today, having sex out of wedlock, took on new importance.

And, of course, we learn that Mariana, the woman the Child sings to, was in fact jilted by Lord Angelo. The righteous deputy now in charge is guilty of breaching a promise of marriage. Would it be that far off base to assume that the mysterious Child in the scene was Angelo's, born out of wedlock? In a play focused on exploring hypocrisy of those who judge, could Angelo be lashing out at others for having sex out of wedlock because he himself had done the same thing? This is certainly a very human behavior pattern, especially among people with power.

I decided to make all the "invisible" children in this story very visible and force their fathers to deal with them. At the end of the play, I decided the Child would reappear with Mariana; my own daughter, an eager six-year-old, could play the role and add another female to the cast, though in prisons we'd have to use a large doll. And our female stage manager could appear for a moment as Kate Keepdown, Lucio's prostitute, holding their toddler (also a puppet), and Julietta could appear holding out the bundle of her newborn child to its father, Claudio. As an added bonus, such strong visuals would also help to make the details of this complicated story clearer.

In addition to wanting to honor my all-female audiences, my imaginings about the script were also affected by knowing that we would be performing at our first men's prison. With *Measure for Measure* I'd decided it was time to take this plunge. As always, my preconceptions of a brand-new audience were in some part based on my initial ignorance and fears. Performing a play that explored sexual power in a men's prison felt a little dangerous. I imagined the men might be open and honest about their misogyny—simply because honesty had been an inherent part of all our nontraditional audiences thus far. This made me want to advocate for the female characters in the play even more strongly; I felt protective of them and the actresses playing them.

In particular, I wondered what the men would make of Lord Angelo's sexual advances on Isabella. I worried that they might take his side and cheer him on. I also worried that by the time we got to the scene where Isabella tells her brother Claudio that it's better that he be executed than she give in and have sex with Angelo, the men would truly despise her. Our Isabella was going to be fierce, intelligent, and opinionated, choosing to enter a nunnery in part to escape men, freeing herself from their condescension and constant sexual advances. But her assertion that "More than our brother is our chastity" was certainly not an easy one to stomach, especially, I imagined, for an audience of all men.

And, of course, imagining the play through the eyes of women did not by any means make me want to gloss over the imperfections, difficulties, and blind spots of the female characters. One of the many blessings of knowing that your audience will truly contain everyone—people of all races, ages, and especially class—is that you can't take sides. Contemplating such an array of audiences makes it clearer than ever that Shakespeare doesn't take sides either—or at least his writing makes it possible not to take sides. His writing is like a crystal, enabling us to see the world through the multiple lenses equally. Or as British theater and film director Peter Brook so elegantly put it, "Shakespeare has no authorship or personal expression; his writing is not a series of messages, but a series of impulses that can produce many understandings."

In *Measure for Measure* especially, there are no complete heroes or complete villains; every character has his or her flaws. In court, Isabella constantly admonishes Angelo to put himself in another's place before he passes judgment: "I would to heaven I had your potency and you were Isabella. Should it then be thus? No, I would tell what 'twere to be a judge, and what a prisoner." But when push comes to shove, Isabella is completely unable to put herself in her brother Claudio's place when he pleads with her to imagine what it feels like to be condemned to die.

Giving all characters equal weight, as I gave all my audiences equal weight, meant that Angelo, of course, could not simply be a villain. I wanted to be fair and sympathetic to him, too, knowing that many men would have found themselves in the position of lusting after someone forbidden, acting on their impulses and regretting it. Angelo's remorse at the end of the play had to be utterly sincere and repentant, opening up this possibility for the men in the audience, even if they hadn't felt repentant before.

PARING DOWN TO THE ESSENCE Angelo hated the sexual part of himself so much that he completely shut himself off from the memory of what he had done with Mariana. Thus closed down, he could not empathize with Claudio or anyone else who had had sex outside of marriage. I started to see that the inability to put oneself in another's place was a problem faced by almost every single character in the play. No one, not Isabella, not the Duke, and certainly not Angelo, seemed to be very good at it. I realized this could be the "spine" of the play—every character at one point or another is asked to put himself in another's place, with varying degrees of success. It is crucial to me when working on a script to pare it down to its essence, which in theater is best expressed as an action. Some also call it a "spine." It's a common action that every single character seems to be trying to do, to one degree or another. A strong spine is another affirmation of our common humanity. Paring a story down to find the spine gives the play a shape that the audience can somehow more easily grasp. The most potent spine is an action that is not only what all the characters in the play are trying to do but what you sense the audience is also grappling with in their actual lives at the time.

Discovering this particular spine in the play was exciting to me because putting yourself in someone else's place is the fundamental activity of theater. It's what we ask actors to do when they work on characters and what we ask our audiences to do as they watch a play. And, of course, I tried to keep doing it with my audiences as I worked on the script, also with varying degrees of success.

ALL CLASSES EQUAL Knowing that people of all classes would be in my audience also helped me to approach each and every character with as much humanity and respect as possible when making choices about them. Again, I found that Shakespeare's writing usually made my task easier. It certainly was not an option to mock or make fun of lower-class characters any more than wealthier characters could be completely vilified for having money and being shortsighted. Prostitutes and barkeeps must have a certain dignity as working people just trying to find a way to get by. Mistress Overdone could not be a silly floozy, despite her name. She was simply a businesswoman, trying to make a living in a world where that is still a hard thing for a woman on her own to do. Lucio, whose witty and honest commentary I imagined the audience would really appreciate, is described as "a fantastic" in the character list, but I chose to make him of the lower classes, earthily rather than extravagantly dressed. I felt it would make him still more accessible to nontraditional audiences, a guy scraping by on the streets who had seen it all and wasn't afraid of anything. And of course we had to give upper-class characters—the Duke, Angelo, and Escalus—the same humanity and respect, not only because we'd be performing for the general public but because the point is to make it as hard as possible to take sides in order that the questions in the play be kept alive. That constant tension of starting to side with one character and then running into a flaw is what makes "the inert lump of coal" that is Shakespeare's writing give off heat and light. Much of my script work is about a kind of constant balancing and rebalancing so that we can see the positives and negatives of every character, not just to be fair but because it makes everything so much more interesting.

ENTERING INTO UNKNOWING   As we headed into rehearsal, I decided to, well, not exactly lie, but at least not admit to the cast that this was my first time directing Shakespeare. I wanted to seem to be an authority; I wanted the actors to trust and have confidence in me. Ever since, though, I have always readily admitted my ignorance and lack of expertise to my casts. I've become confident that *not knowing* is the best place from which to approach Shakespeare. Not only does it help to put the actors at ease, allowing us all to make mistakes and be foolish, but most important it helps us put ourselves in the audience's place of not understanding anything that is going on.

I knew that my first challenge in rehearsal would be to help the actors find

ALL THE LIGHTS ON

stakes for their characters that were high enough. I had learned from past productions that a lot of actors tended to make less urgent, more moderate choices, thinking they were somehow "more interesting." Again, our imagined audiences helped us to quickly get to the high stakes of almost any situation. We knew that many might themselves be prostitutes or barkeeps or pimps or prison guards or even judges. For example, we imagined much more fully the utter desperation of Mistress Overdone when she learns that Angelo has decreed that her business, the brothel, will have to be shut down. We could better imagine the frightening reality of suddenly having no means of support. We found new urgency and depth in the scene where Pompey, her barkeep, tries to reassure her that all will be well. None of this "seriousness" in any way detracted from the characters' humor—people in desperate straits often turn to quite dark humor as a release. Finding the highest stakes possible doesn't make everything grim; it just intensifies everything, including the humor, driving the momentum of each scene.

Then it came time to "not know." After working with the actors for several weeks on the stakes of their situations and figuring out the strongest possible actions they could try to take in the light of such dire circumstances, there came a point where I needed to back away. I had to clear my mind of everything and sit in the audience as someone who knew nothing about what was going on. As I watched scenes from this position of complete ignorance, my mind filled with questions. Who is that guy who just walked onstage? What is everyone blathering on about? What just happened? Why did that guy make the other guys leave the stage and where are they going? Where did that woman come from? Wait, why did that guy just get angry? Shakespeare, for all his splendor, is not always the clearest storyteller.

Some storytelling problems were fairly easily solved. Characters often used pronouns instead of names when they were talking, so I didn't really understand who they were talking about. Sometimes there were two or three different pronouns in the same sentence, each one referring to a different person! This of course was easily fixed by inserting actual names. Sometimes this didn't quite fit with the scansion, but I figured understanding the story was more important.

I also noticed that characters often talked about people or events offstage that I couldn't see. Without some kind of visual anchor in the sea of floating, unattached words, it was actually very hard to understand who or what was being talked about. This was often simply solved by having characters gesture or point to where the character had last been seen or where we understood the event might be taking place. I am not a fan of actors who make heavy use of hand gestures to act out words; I find it condescending and often ultimately confusing. But pointing to help us understand offstage events can be such a huge and welcome relief. One simple gesture can unlock a tumble of words; one pointing finger and, amazingly, all becomes clear. We've now embraced this concept thoroughly, referring to it as "The Ten Thousand Things Pointing School of Acting."

THE NEED FOR LOTS OF MOVEMENT And even when the story was fairly clear when reading the actual words of the text, when the actors spoke onstage, I still often just heard a bunch of words without having any real idea what anyone was actually saying. I began to realize that when words washed over me, more often than not it was because the action underlying the words of the character was not strong and clear. It's such a basic directing rule, hammered away at incessantly in directing school—every time a character speaks, he or she is trying to *do* something to the person they are talking to. We are all taught that there's always a very active subtext underneath anyone's words. No matter what a character is saying, we were taught to look for what he or she is really *doing*, whether it's dismissing, or embracing, or pushing away, or seducing. If an action is strong and clear, you can feel it viscerally, no matter the language. So it was surprising to me how often, when I watched other Shakespeare productions, I couldn't feel the actions of the characters underneath their speeches. Feeling those actions helps so much to make sense of the words. With *Measure for Measure*, I realized I needed this play of amazing language, in a funny way, to be "language proof"—so you could understand it even if you couldn't understand the words.

I also noticed that it became harder for me to understand what characters were saying whenever they stood still for a long time. Stillness seemed to be

ALL THE LIGHTS ON

a big part of Shakespeare, especially during long speeches. I saw quickly how movement could help so much to understand a character's words, especially if it mirrored the action underneath. If the Duke at the beginning of the story was trying to throw all her colleagues off balance, surprise them, and get out of town as quickly as she could, her movements as she spoke could reflect this. She could head toward the door and then suddenly come back in for a bit of further instruction before heading out the door again, darting back and forth quickly as she spoke. Movement could help us understand how a character's thinking was unfolding, too, pacing as she worked to figure out a problem, stopping or starting suddenly as a new idea occurred. If Angelo, talking alone onstage, was trying to figure out a way to handle his lust, his movements could reflect his thinking, with a change of direction every time he changed the direction of his thoughts. The stops, starts, and changes of direction could break up those long speeches, helping us physically to understand his thought processes and discoveries of new ideas.

Sometimes veteran Shakespearean actors new to the company have resisted this kind of movement while speaking, worrying that it will be too "illustrative" or perhaps condescending. But once they are plunged into the heat of the immediacy of a Ten Thousand Things performance, that concern rapidly vanishes. All anyone wants is to have the story be clear. I have never encountered an audience, whether first timers or veterans, who felt that this kind of movement was too simplistic. Rather, all have seemed to find whatever help they can get in understanding the onslaught of words rushing toward them as a relief. They can spend their energies entering into the depths of the play rather than have to waste them by trying to clear away their confusion.

I began to see how, with so little else to fall back on in terms of set, lighting, or props, movement was actually our best tool for creating clarity, helping the audience to understand the actions under the words as characters spoke, approached, or retreated, underscoring their shifting needs toward one another. Almost never in a Ten Thousand Things production of any kind does a character stand still for more than a minute (and almost never does one sit), as it robs us of the chance for movement, the chance to get some further understanding into what is really going on onstage. Audiences quickly grow restless when actors stand still and declaim—or wallow.

I had noticed during our previous tours that audiences became quite restless whenever a character paused to emote. Certainly many of their own lives, so often focused around daily survival, afforded little time for emotional wallowing. If the stakes of a situation are truly urgent, people don't have the luxury of time to sit around and feel things. Action needs to be taken. Action, not emotion, is the building material of theater for good reason, and the restlessness of our audiences whenever a character took too long a pause in what he or she was doing to just "feel things" helped to strongly underscore this. We needed to keep things moving.

THE LANGUAGE COMES LAST Then, finally in rehearsals, I turned my attention to the language. I know this seems strange, perhaps even heretical to some Shakespeare artists, who so often *start* with the language. Certainly the actors, many skilled in scansion and meter, had been aware of and working with it as a tool all along. But I only paid attention to the language once the stakes and the actions were very strong and clear. It was like I was coming up for air, having watched everything underwater to be sure I could feel the actions in my gut. Only then did I come up to listen to the actual words. When I still couldn't understand exactly what people were saying, I often found that all that was needed was a little tweaking, perhaps just a little stronger emphasis on a certain word, and then the whole sentence would become clear. I didn't apply any external formulas or rules about how Shakespeare was supposed to be spoken. I just listened for what I needed to know to understand the story and made little adjustments to emphasis or rhythm or speed to bring clarity.

At this point, I'd also notice what words didn't seem "full enough." It really stood out if an actor was rushing through the words, taking them all for granted as he spoke. It was also a signal that the actor might not have gone deeply enough into the stakes of his situation so that he could truly fill up the words. In addition to urging more depth, I challenged the actors to grapple with how the strange and beautiful words were forged in the belly of necessity, each particular one arising because it was absolutely needed at that moment to help the character *do* whatever he or she was trying to do. It was a gift to be given the ability as a human being to find the most powerful words. Finally, at the very end of the rehearsal process, I could embrace the joy and delight of the language, helping the actors, in the places they hadn't been able to yet, to do the same.

A SHAKESPEARE EPIPHANY   And thus, armed with our attempts to imagine the characters and story through our audience's eyes—the high stakes, the strong actions, our clear and urgent story, the amazing and necessary words—we set out to meet our first audience. We made a circle of chairs at the Dorothy Day Center in downtown St. Paul, Minnesota, an enormous space for the homeless to drop in during the day, to hang out, stay warm, have a cup of coffee and conversation. Gradually, about sixty people filled the two rows. We were all terrified. I honestly did not know if they would be able to follow this complex story with its unfamiliar language. But all we could do at that point was take the plunge. And at this very first performance, we had what we now refer to as "our Shakespeare epiphany."

I began by making a brief introduction to the story, setting the stage so it would be easier to enter. I also took a moment to reassure everyone that even people who have seen lots of Shakespeare before always find it challenging to understand what's going on at first because the language is so different from what we're used to hearing, but that after five or ten minutes, everything should become clear. After the first few scenes, the audience seemed to be pretty engaged, following the story, as best we could tell. Indeed, as time passed, I got my first clear sense that the spareness of our staging, the lack of objects and set pieces on the stage, actually made it much easier for everyone to focus on the language, heightening it and allowing all to take pleasure in it.

Then we came to the courtroom scene where Isabella pleads with the rigid, puritanical deputy Angelo to spare her brother's life, unsure of herself at first but coming up with an arsenal of fierce arguments as the scene progresses. Angelo, somehow moved, asks her to leave and return the next day for an answer. He is left alone onstage to wrestle with the feelings that Isabella has produced in him. "What's this? What's this? The tempted or the temptress, who sins most?" he asks.

And at that moment, an older woman sitting less than a foot away from Angelo, played by the very experienced Shakespearean actor Steve Hendrickson in his first ever Ten Thousand Things performance, looked him directly in the eyes and said, "I think it's your fault, shithead." Everyone seated around her began to laugh. Then a man standing at the back of the room shouted out, "Oh, go ahead and fuck her!" The entire audience burst into hoots and guffaws. Steve began to panic. He told us later that he felt like he had completely lost the crowd and didn't know how to get them back. Then he thought of his next line. All he had to do was say it. "Not she, nor does she tempt, but tis I." A conversation with the audience was born.

We suddenly remembered the groundlings, the people who paid a penny for a ticket, who stood in front of the stage at the Globe and shouted remarks at the actors. Shakespeare wrote his plays *expecting* them to shout back to his characters. A "soliloquy" was not a quiet solitary moment for a character to speak his thoughts aloud. It was an active conversation with the audience, with people shouting out advice and judgments—just as they had at our first performance of *The Good Person* and at so many other performances since then. That's when we truly realized that Shakespeare did write for *everyone*, not just the polite, quiet, wealthy, and well-educated patrons sitting in box seats. To write such conversations he must have known his audience, both rich and poor, well enough to imagine what they would say in response. Our performance at the homeless drop-in center was a visceral confirmation of this simple fact. He, like us, must have been holding his audience in mind as he wrote.

Our audience at the Hennepin County Women's Correctional Facility was even livelier; the women openly booed and cheered on the characters. These women gave us the answer to that problem that had always troubled me in *Measure for Measure*. They taught us how to understand Isabella's choice of her "chastity" over her brother's life. This audience was all too familiar with Isabella's situation, completely alone and at the mercy of a powerful man. They immediately knew what Angelo was up to with his request for Isabel-

Steve Hendrickson played Angelo in *Measure for Measure* at the Dorothy Day Center in 1998.

la to return the next day; they began to hiss and catcall. They were fiercely on Isabella's side. They understood completely what was at stake in this scene, and religious conviction was the least of it. What Angelo was asking for wasn't "just sex." It was rape. Pure and simple. It was a horrible violation, an act of brute force, no matter how politely it was couched. The cloaking of Isabella's feelings in religious garb and the use of the word "chastity" somehow served to diminish the violence of it all. Seeing this situation through the eyes of women who had been there themselves suddenly made the balance between the horror of Claudio's looming execution and Isabella's looming rape much more balanced. These women finally showed us how to take Isabella's situation in all its full seriousness, in a way we had not been able to imagine before.

In the years following, I have had the chance to bring *Measure for Measure* on several other tours (including one for the Public Theater in New York City, which wanted to experience our model). The reactions to the Angelo/Isabella scenes are always visceral in the women's prisons, but they aren't always quite the same. There are differences even according to the type of prison. Isabella has a "soliloquy moment" in the play, too, when she returns to court the next day to receive the ruling about her brother. Angelo presents her with a stark choice—the only way to spare your brother is to let me rape you. Left alone to process this impossible situation, Isabella asks, "To whom should I complain? Should I tell this, who would believe me?" In a minimum-security jail in Manhattan, the women indignantly shouted out advice: "Call the police! That guy's an asshole!" But in a maximum-security prison outside the city, complete silence greeted Isabella's question. The silence was very full, and the actress let it linger. After a moment, a sole voice spoke out quietly: "That's what it's like. No one to listen."

I don't know how Shakespeare intended this scene to be played. I don't think it's possible to know. I was able to see a production by London's Globe Theater, with an all-male cast, just as it was cast in Shakespeare's time. Isabella was played by a lanky young man, and both she and Angelo came across as ridiculous and uptight prudes. That certainly might have resonated with Shakespeare's audiences, and it also seemed to do so with the largely liberal

ALL THE LIGHTS ON

Nathan Barlow as Claudio, *Measure for Measure*, Project Success, 2012.

upper-middle-class audience who watched the play, resonating as a way to skewer the hypocrisy of many right-wing Christian fundamentalists. All I know is that with our larger audiences who have lived at the edges, many of whom haven't the time to be involved in the political discussion of the day, we have to take a different approach to mirror the truth of their lives. We must approach things first and foremost at a deeply personal level. Artistic choices made out of necessity, once again.

ALL-MALE AUDIENCES   Turning back to that very first tour, we finally came to our anxiously anticipated, first-ever men's prison audience. As I looked out at the rings of chairs filled by very large men in gray sweats and black Converse sneakers, slouched in their seats with arms folded, defying us to entertain them, I experienced yet another "you must be out of your mind" moment. I looked at the actress playing Isabella, Signe Albertson. She was clearly feeling the same way.

The first unexpected surprise was the audience's complete embrace of Shakespeare's bawdy humor. I had never heard an audience laugh so hard at Shakespeare. No glossary or footnotes were needed for the men to pick up the sexual innuendo contained in the lines between Pompey and Mistress Overdone and Lucio. They even caught a few that we had missed! The laughter was deep and hearty, pure enjoyment of the ability to hear such things said in a prison, under the watch of the guards (who were themselves smiling), and appreciation of the actors for being so honest. Any audience who has been deprived of sex for many months, we quickly learned, will thoroughly relish the slightest hint of it. Our prison audiences have helped us to understand that most theater is really in some way about sexual energy, about the tensions produced by live bodies on display, interacting onstage.

Then came the dreaded scenes between Isabella and Angelo. Talking about sexuality and a possible rape felt dangerous in that gym full of men. But our fears that the men would side with Angelo and just see Isabella as an object of lust were soon put to rest. Most of the men did quickly recognize Angelo's intentions, smiling at the subtext they could feel beneath his polite arguments and language. But we also started to sense a protectiveness toward Isabella. It became clear that many of the men were identifying with her as they might with a younger sister who found herself in a vulnerable situation. It was actually easier for them to take her side than the side of a white male authority figure, a judge perhaps not unlike the ones who had sentenced them to jail. In the next scene, where Claudio begs his sister to imagine what he must feel like, being condemned to death, the men were clearly sympathetic to Claudio and didn't view the plights as equal. But they did not seem to reject or ridicule Isabella for her passionate defense of her chastity. Our fears had been our own. Our assumptions had not at all been correct.

And then, in the final scene of the play, when Claudio miraculously appears to Isabella, who has been led to believe that her brother has been killed, I looked around the audience and saw tears in the eyes of some of the inmates. I was startled. The men seemed to be deeply identifying with Claudio, longing

ALL THE LIGHTS ON

for their own moment of reunion with a family member or loved one. I could never remember seeing tears in the eyes of any audience watching Shakespeare, ever. This story was the story of the audience's *lives*.

Afterward, we were lucky to be able to have a conversation with some of the inmates (this is not always possible in jail). One man commented, "I'm getting out tomorrow. I didn't know theater was like this. I'm going to take my kid." Another inmate turned out to be a Shakespearean scholar from South Africa who had enjoyed the performance very much and appreciated our casting

Luverne Seifert as Pompey, *Measure for Measure*, Project Success, 2012.

of a woman as the Duke. And one inmate eloquently offered, "This is my first taste of Shakespeare and I hunger for more."

Finally, we brought the show to paying customers for three performances at a somewhat rickety dance space on the second floor of a building in downtown Minneapolis. Perhaps almost as gratifying as the response of our nontraditional audiences to our Shakespearean work has been the response of those who pay for their tickets. We now do four weekends, or sixteen performances of every show, for the general public, usually selling out quickly. It seems that this stripped-down, fierce, clear, and intimate style of doing Shakespeare is speaking to people who have seen a lot of theater. So many people have told us it's the best Shakespeare they've ever seen, that for the first time they have been truly able to understand and connect with the stories going on. I believe audiences now, used to close-ups of actors' faces on television and film, are hungering for the same closeness in theater so they can read the details of actors' facial movements. They want to see actors who don't have to strain to project emotions to the back of large auditoriums. They hunger for the jarring intimacy you feel close to live bodies radiating enormous and truthful emotions. Because these veteran audiences seem so grateful that the story is clear, the language is accessible, the momentum is rapid, the depth and truth of the acting so profound, and the details so easily visible, it makes me think that perhaps some of those things have not been available to them in the Shakespeare they've seen elsewhere. Creating Shakespeare by holding in mind an audience that includes every sort of human being seems to enrich and enliven the experience for all.

For most of the seasons following this first experience, we have included a Shakespeare play, ranging from an all-male *Richard III* to an all-female *Twelfth Night*. We've performed his comedies and tragedies and each time used the multifaceted lenses of our many audiences with which to view the multifaceted dimensions of his plays. We don't need to have a "concept" or choose a historical setting like 1930s Cuba or 1960s sitcoms to make the plays come to life. Each time, through necessity, the simple act of imagining our audiences makes most of the artistic choices for us. We often just look for one large and simple territory to explore with each play, as a focus for our work but also

ALL THE LIGHTS ON

because many of the plays, for all their complexity, seem to have been written that way. *Richard III* is a play about being an outcast in the world, and certainly a situation most in our nontraditional audiences can relate to. *The Tempest* becomes a story where every character struggles with the very human need for revenge. *Othello* is a play whose characters each wrestle with jealousy on a spectrum. Yes, these one-word emotional territories seem simple and obvious—but jealousy or revenge or judgment each provide an endlessly fertile, deep, and complex terrain to explore. Such a clear and simple demarcation lends a focus to our storytelling and allows the audience to consider these fundamental human conditions from all angles, which can be exhilarating. You don't need to get much fancier.

Shakespeare wrote plays knowing that *everyone* would be in his audience. It seems the most pressing Shakespearean work we can do today is to attempt to tell the stories again, clearly and deeply, to an audience that also truly contains everyone. Though to many this may seem daunting, it is an exciting charge, fraught with creative possibility, and I believe necessary for those who hope to keep Shakespeare's work living into the future.

Bubbles for *The Emperor of the Moon* finale, Dorothy Day Center, 1997.

ABBONDANZA! THE WEALTH OF VERY FEW THINGS
Production Values

MORE THAN TWENTY YEARS after making the *Good Person* set from cloth cutouts, cardboard barrels, two ropes, and a few boards, using that little bag of silver from my mom, we still have never spent more than one thousand dollars on set supplies for any show. There are several very good reasons for this, but the most important is the primary principle of Ten Thousand Things design: "Yeah, but do you wanna carry it?" Our sets must be carried down long hallways, lugged up long staircases, crammed into elevators, and heaved in and out of our small rented cargo van. Out of such necessity, we have our defining aesthetic.

We are certainly not the only theater company with an aesthetic of using minimal set pieces and very few props. Many other wonderful theater artists choose "empty space" over a detailed rendering of time and place when creating their work. But working in a bare-bones style for so many years because we *must*, as well as performing for so many audiences who also find themselves with very few material possessions has given us a unique perspective from which to see the abundance that comes from having very few things.

At first, the cinderblock walls and linoleum floors or industrial carpeting, in hues of beige and gray, that make up the world in which many in our audiences spend a great deal of their time seemed like something to try to overcome. I believe that all of us have a hunger for beauty, and I wanted to try to use our sets to transform these dreary spaces. For *Electra*, our second show, I worked with the designer to make some simple, light canvas flats that glowed with mysterious blues and greens, hoping they would somehow cover up whatever drab room in the juvenile prisons we might find ourselves in. But the painted flats actually just heightened the surrounding dinginess. The cold, industrial rooms overwhelmed the little set and made things somehow even bleaker.

As with everything else, it took me a while to process all this. With our next show, *Life's a Dream* (still performed proscenium style in front of rows of chairs), I again tried to blot out the room. We hung large, brightly colored cloths on a rod frame behind the actors to make a backdrop. And, once again, this didn't transform anything; it all just looked sorry when viewed against the bleak space. I finally started to understand that the only way to transform a room would be through the imagination of the audience—not through covering it up with things.

Our first foray into comedy came soon after. The raucous laughter of our audiences at comic moments in the plays we'd done so far helped me understand how rare and precious a thing laughter can be for people who are living very hard lives, so I thought we'd try a whole play devoted to it. Carlo Gozzi's seventeenth-century fantasy *The King Stag* attracted my attention. In an early attempt to wrestle with the horrible sexism of this particular classical play, I tried reversing the gender of all the roles (I would now recommend against this!) and retitled it *The Queen Stag*. I still wanted the play to grapple with a struggle in the lives of our audiences somehow; the play seemed to be wrestling with the way we so often confuse people's appearance with the nature of their souls. I thought that might resonate with many in our audience who are so often judged on their appearance. I honestly don't know if anyone connected with that issue while they watched the play—but they certainly all did end up laughing a lot.

I was also attracted to this wildly fanciful story of transmigrating souls because of the challenge of its scenic "requirements." The play takes place in magical forests and palaces; to do so "realistically," by filling in all the empty space with actual full-size forests and castles, would be impossible, of course, so I went to the other extreme. To set the scene, an actor just ran across the playing space trailing a long green piece of fabric, whispering "Forest, forest, forest." And when the setting changed, a long gold piece of cloth was whisked across, with another whispered prompt, "Palace, palace, palace." The audience

ALL THE LIGHTS ON

was delighted with the invitation and willingly jumped right in to imagine. The forests and palaces they created themselves were likely much more wonderful than anything we could have made by ourselves. (That set remains one of my very favorites because it was the *lightest;* just pieces of cloth we folded up and carried effortlessly to our cars.)

From that point on, I heartily embraced the limitations of Ten Thousand Things staging. I had always instinctively been drawn toward the theater of empty space anyway, so it was an easy match. Instead of trying to create a world with set pieces and objects, I wanted to find the least we would need to prompt the audience to create their own worlds. I began to relish tackling seemingly impossible staging challenges with as little as possible.

SETS I knew that with at least some of the plays we did, I wanted to continue to explore the territory of joy. I was on the lookout for stories about wily servants deceiving their masters, stories that in some way at least made room for different perspectives of class, and, always, a female point of view. All these elements came together when I stumbled on *The Emperor of the Moon,* by England's first woman playwright, Aphra Behn. This wildly ridiculous story, about using trickery and subterfuge against the powers that be to claim one's own true love, has immense staging challenges. In the finale, when all the loving pairs are correctly united at last, Behn calls for

> *The Hill of Parnassus; a noble large walk of trees leading to it with eight or ten Negroes upon Pedestals, ranged on each side. Next Keplair and Gailieus descend on each side in Chariots with Perspectives in their hands. Next the Zodiack descends, a Symphony playing all the while; when it is landed it delivers the twelve Signs: then the Song, the Persons of the Zodiack being the singers. After which the Globe of the Moon appears, first like a new Moon, as it moves forward it increases till it comes to the Full. When it is descended it opens and shews the Emperor and the Prince, who come forth with all their Train born by Cupids, the Flutes playing a Symphony before them.*

I relished the challenge. I needed to translate such excess into something simple and expressive of the play's joyous spirit. The spheres and globes of the planets and moons suggested bubbles. I discovered I could rent three bubble machines for a few weeks for less than a hundred dollars. We hid them in painted boxes, and at the moment of the grand finale, we switched them on. Hundreds of bubbles filled the tired spaces of shelters and prisons, floating over the audience's heads and popping into their faces, all to the sound of a wailing saxophone. So much joy and delight from a bubble, much more, I think, than any elaborate set could ever have created.

With more productions under my belt, I began to work with a sculptor whose ways of thinking about materials and objects were much different from those of many set designers. Theatrical designers are accustomed to making "fake things" and transforming them with various tricks of paint and lighting (lighting, of course, that we didn't have). I wanted the set pieces we brought into our production spaces to be beautiful in and of themselves; I felt they could also be more abstract as well as more artful. I was drawn to a sculptor, Stephen Mohring, who worked with bare wood and metal. Though I couldn't have articulated this at the time, it felt better to just be honest about where we were and what little we had. I thought we would draw in the audience even more strongly by giving them the sparest suggestions of place, without paint or much color, inviting them to transform a few objects that in their starkness were actually quite beautiful.

Measure for Measure, in 1998, was the first play Stephen and I started working on together to develop this aesthetic. Always interested in economy and carrying less, we began to explore the possibilities of having each set piece function as many different things. I craved simple shapes, a world made of just circles or just rectangles. With *Measure for Measure*, the scales of justice came to mind, and their triangular shape permeated my thinking. Black steel tubing could form the outlines of triangles: waist-high triangles could be gates in the prison or podiums in the court, a few triangular-peaked archways on wheels could be entrances to court or to a monastery, a triangular metal stool for a garden bench or a seat in the prison waiting room. The sounds of clanging metal could help to shape the percussive pace of the play. Using one shape to become many different things helped to create a separate world that was very different from our everyday one, or any historically accurate one,

Measure for Measure set pieces by Stephen Mohring.

and it created a coherence to the made-up world. Even more important, the single shape allowed us to start to see connections between otherwise very separate worlds of prisons, churches, and courts.

WHAT TO WEAR   With *Measure for Measure*, we started refining our ideas about costuming, too. Because set pieces take up so little space, costumes are really what create the fullness of our worlds, their color and texture. I found myself drawn away from theatrically trained costume designers, who so often are oriented to creating an individuality for each character, giving each one a distinctive color and shape to differentiate them from everyone else. I wanted to make up a coherent world, and that meant exploring what the characters shared in common. My interest turned toward fiber artists, who easily plunged into the spirit of such work.

We sensed that by strictly limiting the palette of color used for all the costumes, we could create a strong visual unity. The harsh world of *Measure for Measure* drew us to blacks and grays, matching the steel tubing, with hints of tan and brown to match the few pieces of bare wood in the set. The textile artist, Ellen Hutchinson, and I went to a large fabric warehouse looking for cloth that seemed to belong in the world of the play. We pulled bolts from the shelves with glee and spread them on a big table to consider. We relished being able to really make use of texture. Because our audience sits so close with no lighting to get in the way, the actual textures of the fabrics can really be seen and appreciated. Within our strict color palette, with everyone dressed in the same colors, texture would be the way to distinguish the economic circumstances of a character—coarser, rougher cloth for those of lower classes; shinier, smoother embossed fabric for those of means. Yet I didn't want such distinctions to be strict. We treated the array of bolts we had chosen as the universe of available fabrics in the world. Characters might share some fabrics—one might have a vest and another a skirt made of the same cloth. Sometimes a small piece of coarse fabric might appear in the costume of a wealthier person, and a poorer character might have a scrap of shiny fabric he'd patched into his sleeve. As with the beauty of the sculpted bare wood and metal set pieces, texture in the fabric of the costumes was a way we could pull in the audience to notice the beauty of the simple materials directly in front of them.

We also looked for coherence in the shapes of the clothes. Ellen thought nothing of sewing all the pieces from scratch, so we were able to choose one or two strange shapes, perhaps balloon pants and long tunics, that most everyone could wear, no matter their economic circumstances. Unusual shape, unconnected to any specific historical period, along with a strictly limited color palette and a universe of fabrics shared among all characters became the simplest way to make our fairy tale worlds. Already limited by what we could carry, we chose to restrict ourselves even more, by shape, color, and tex-

ALL THE LIGHTS ON

ture. Out of these limitations we could invite our audience in to help us create worlds from times and places no one had ever experienced before, worlds in which no one was the expert.

Such strong visual coherence helps to satisfy the other absolute necessity of Ten Thousand Things performance situations: creating focus. Remember that we have no elevated stage, no stage lighting, no spotlights, no dark house—none of the usual theatrical tools for creating focus. The spaces are often large and chaotic, sometimes with lines of other people in the room waiting for health care or for food. Soda machines hum, bulletin boards and brightly colored posters adorn the walls, phones ring and announcements come suddenly over loudspeakers. Our audiences are often skeptical or uncertain, distracted by larger issues in their lives. As artists, we must strive with all our might to create the strongest focus we can, for each and every minute of the play. A powerful visual coherence to our sets and costumes is one way to help with this. And the strong invitation to the audience to help create the world with us also harnesses otherwise scattered energy.

THE CIRCLE OF AUDIENCE Having the audience define the edges of our stage has become another crucial way to create focus, but again, it took me five or six productions to discover this. Our one disastrous experience with an actual stage when we had to do *Life's a Dream* for the youth at risk at the church showed us what an enormous barrier a stage's elevation can be for people who have never experienced theater before. After that I vowed to always perform on the floor, on the same level as our audiences, even if a stage was available. But for a few more shows, we continued to play proscenium style in front of rows of chairs. It wasn't until Brecht's *The Caucasian Chalk Circle* that I stumbled upon the idea of performing in the round. A circle. It's in the title. Once again the discovery came out of necessity. The story of Grusha, the palace kitchen maid, and the abandoned child she decides to care for, requires them to journey all over the war-torn countryside. The thought of conveying all this traveling back and forth across the straight lines of a proscenium stage seemed very tiresome. I finally realized that if we performed in the round, with a few aisles radiating from the center, Grusha could move around the

Ragtime curtain at women's correctional center, 2005.

outside of the circle behind the audience. The focus on the story would also be sustained if the audience could watch her travel around between the scenes.

A circle offered many other benefits. The edges of the whole playing area would now be completely defined by the audience or, even more precisely, the tension between the actors and the audience. The actors could break that tension by traveling into the four radiating aisles in the "corners" of the circle as well as the space behind the chairs. At times the play could completely surround the audience. The circle could always be the same size, so our stage could always be twelve to fifteen feet across, no matter what the size of the room. We almost never have more than three rows of chairs ringing the stage. Actors might be inches away from an audience member, almost never further than a dozen feet. In addition, the circle of audience members would all be able to see each other's faces, fully lit, not just dark silhouettes of the backs of heads, as is the case in a conventional theater. In-the-round staging also encourages a multiplicity of viewpoints and perspectives. Sometimes an actor's back is to us and we must imagine her facial expression, or sometimes when our view is temporarily blocked by an actor we can look at an audience member seated across the stage and imagine how things look from her point of view. Plus, practically speaking, this kind of staging allowed us to quadruple the number of people who could sit in the front row. All of these factors greatly intensified the quality of the audience's attention. We've performed in a circle or a square ever since.

ALL THE LIGHTS ON

But all of these efforts to create focus—strong visual coherence from limited palettes of shape and color, inviting the audience in to help create the world with their imaginations, completely surrounding the play with the audience and the audience with the play—are still not enough for us to be able to tell a story clearly.

YOU MUST HAVE SOUND   Live sound is as critical to creating focus in our work as lighting instruments are in the regular theater. We always have live sound for every production. A gong, a chime, a drum, a dissonant chord, or a ukulele twang can create a spotlight, a color, a transition, or a blackout—in full fluorescent light. And as the multitalented actor/musician/singer/composer Peter Vitale and I have learned over the years, to create focus with such "lighting," *sound* is preferable to music. Musical interludes often have a precise emotional content and so tend to shape our feelings. Percussion and unfamiliar, unspecific sounds allow listeners more emotional space and flexibility. This important difference sets Peter's work apart from that of more traditional "sound designers." Rather than highlighting the mood or emotion of a scene, our sound tends to *punctuate the action* onstage. We use it to draw the audience's attention to exits, to entrances, to key moments, helping to make the story clear rather than telling them what to feel.

AND IT HAS TO BE LIVE   Live sound creates a vital energy that prerecorded sounds can never approach. Taped sounds, as I learned frantically punching the buttons on a cassette player in one painful early experience before I met Peter, are deadly. Again, abstract live sounds work best. Rather than actual sounds of doorbells ringing or dogs barking, imaginations are more engaged by strange sounds that suggest these things. We invite the audience to fill in the blanks themselves because, once again, this intensifies their engagement. Peter always sits at the end of one of the four aisles, barely removed from the playing area, surrounded by a dizzying array of acoustic and often invented instruments: drums, wind chimes, whistles, gongs, and mallets, plus strangely welded pieces of metal, with a ukulele, a clarinet, a harp and/or a saxophone thrown in for good measure, depending on the needs of each story. He's become adept at playing two or three sounds at once, or four or five in rapid succession. Occasionally Peter will use the sounds available from an electric keyboard, but we always try at first to see if we can do without because we all hate to carry the amp and electrical cords. We layer the sounds in over the entire course of the rehearsal period, adding and eliminating instruments as we go; the actors love the clarity, depth, and focus these sounds lend and come to depend on them. Peter's live presence in the room, punctuating and heightening the story in the moment with the actors, creates still more energy, immediacy, and edge that compel the audience to enter into the story even more deeply. Our nontraditional audiences often gather with great curiosity around Peter, hanging out before and after performances. They are hungry for live music and sound, some of them even quite literally starved for it.

THE REVELATIONS OF METAPHOR   Already limited by what we can carry and the wildly varied rooms in which we perform, we've learned to embrace still more limits, restricting what little we have even further, in part to create supremely necessary focus. And with this embrace of more limitations, we've uncovered another enormous blessing—the revelations of metaphor. Metaphors allow us to see the connections between things that seem unrelated. In real life, with all its clutter, it's often hard to see these connections. But when theater strips everything down, the connections are all much easier to see.

Take *Richard III*, for example, which we performed with an all-male cast. Hoops were the shape of our few set pieces, props, and costumes—black hoops that seemed to have been pounded out of iron. Five small hoops formed the cross sections of a small skeletal tower—the Tower of London—that could be wheeled into a corner of the circular playing space as a reminder whenever the dreadful prison appeared in the story. Dark hoops were the structure of the female characters' skeletal skirts and corsets, allowing the men's bodies and pants to appear through the frames; such women's clothing suggested how the female characters were also imprisoned and constrained by their roles. Metal hoops formed the structure of the men's armor as well, for warriors are prisoner to the demands of the battlefield. And the crown, another black metal hoop, had five spikes on top of it, just as the top hoop of the Tower did, allowing us to see the connection between a king's role and a prison's constraints. All we offered our audiences to look at were dark metal hoops, but because there was so little, we could more easily see the connections between unrelated things. We could literally see the metaphors, feeling the harshness of the black iron constraints everywhere.

With *The Little Shop of Horrors*, it was easy to see how the story of the struggles of Seymour, the hapless flower shop clerk on skid row, might connect with our audience members. But since we artists were relatively ignorant of the realities of such places, we decided to limit the set materials to rebar and tinfoil, creating an abstract skid row shop that lifted the play out of its reality into more of a fairy tale realm. We were freed from having to replicate

Luverne Seifert, Richard Ooms, and Craig Johnson as the Queens, costumes by Kathy Kohl, *Richard III*, Minnesota Opera Center, 2007.

the details of skid row, and our audiences, in turn, were freed from having to cringe over how we'd gotten the details so wrong. The audience also got some distance from any actual painful skid row experiences they might have had, and everyone could focus on the story at hand instead.

Then there was that giant man-eating plant. To try to believably operate and bring to life—let alone transport—some enormous gaudy puppet big enough to swallow people, especially without the help of any stage lighting or curtains, was clearly ridiculous and impossible. This was, of course, an irresistible challenge. My mind traveled to the very opposite end of the puppet spectrum. A bare hand. Four fingers opening and closing on top of the thumb in a talking beak, the kind every kid makes. We could make a flowerpot out of which grew a metal stem with a loop on top, a loop big enough to stick a hand through. The fabulously physically inventive actor playing Seymour, Jim Lichtscheidl, could just lower his voice and make his bare hand talk whenever the plant did. I knew Jim would relish singing both parts of Seymour's duets with the plant. Every time the plant grew, we could raise the stem higher or move to a bigger pot with a taller stem and bigger loop. A piece of black cloth could cover those who got eaten as the plant grew, and I knew that our particular Seymour would take great delight in figuring out how to get his hand to eat himself at the end.

Without that big gaudy prop of a flower puppet in the way, a metaphor was revealed. Wasn't that big hungry plant just an extension of shy, uncertain Seymour? His suppressed hunger for love and attention an alter ego manifesting itself in a flowerpot? The connection between Seymour and the ravenous man-eating plant became clear, and the childlike theatrical trick delighted the audiences.

Musicals always demand the most in terms of set and props, no matter how much we try to pare things down. We let ourselves go a little wild on such shows, though we still remain, as an actress once declared in a moment of exasperation after being denied a request for a prop, "The Amish Theater Company!" *The Most Happy Fella* tells the story of an unlikely romance growing out of correspondence between an elderly Italian immigrant vineyard owner and a young (in our cast, African American) waitress. Unlikely romance is something we all yearn for, and in our production I wanted to focus on the fears that kept getting in the way of love's blossoming generosity.

Most of the play takes place on a Napa Valley grape ranch. I was drawn to the Y shape of the wooden supports of the vines. They seemed like two generous outspread arms, echoing our exploration of abundance and giving without fear. In addition to supporting vines, the bare wood Y-shapes could support little round tabletops in Rosabella's restaurant as well as the street sign on the town corner where ranch hands stood "watchin' all the girls go by." To create the rows of the vineyard, we made nine wooden Ys and stuck them in bare wood boxes, or planters, on wheels, three in each row across the playing square. Against all this bare wood, we restricted the costumes to a palette of greens and purples, echoing the colors of a vineyard.

The bare wood focused our attention on the vines. We just made them out of bright green string: the vines could "grow" by having actors lift them out of the boxes and drape them over the Y supports. During times of abundance and love, actors could lift out vines growing not only bunches of grapes but little plastic bottles of wine and rounds of cheese and pieces of cake and even—as the pinnacle of our special effects—little round paper lanterns, sparkling with intertwined Christmas lights, all shining with glorious color. In times of fear and deception in the couple's story, actors would cause the vines to shrivel and disappear back into the wooden boxes. Trying to mend their relationship after weeks of misunderstanding, Rosabella and Tony working together in the vineyard might pull up little green shoots of vines from the boxes, helping them to begin to grow on the Y supports once again. Wooden Ys and green strings were all it took to get us to see clearly how the objects in the play, pared down to what was only most essential, could serve as metaphors for the emotions and relationships growing and changing onstage.

Back in the early days, when I was trying to come up with a name for our work, I wanted to avoid anything obvious or condescending like "The Poor People's Theater Company." At the time I was reading a novel about a mysterious island in Indonesia, a strange and beautiful tale called *The Ten Thousand Things* by Maria Dermout. I liked the breadth of imaginative possibility this name

Jim Lichtscheidl as Seymour with his hand as the man-eating plant, *Little Shop of Horrors,*
St. Paul low-income housing, 2007.

presented; it suggested that we could do any kind of theater for any kind of audience. I snatched it up.

Several years later I stumbled upon the phrase again, this time in reference to a Buddhist concept, a way to describe "all the material things in the world." I drew a sharp breath of recognition. I loved how the name corralled all the innumerable material things in the world into a limited space. There were only ten thousand, and no more. I was immediately able to see how most people in our audiences—and we as a theater company—possessed very few of those ten thousand things. Yet we did not think of ourselves as poor. Placing limits around material objects lets us begin to think about what else there is besides those things. Imagination and spirit, fears and hungers, kindness and heart and laughter: these are what connect us all as human beings. When there is not a lot of stuff in the way, somehow these things get easier to see.

So much of my work on a play at Ten Thousand Things is about paring down to the essence. When I'm restricted, by necessity, in the number of things I can put onstage, this also helps to get to essences, to what is truly most important. Having so few things onstage helps us to see the essence of the objects, too: a crown is just a circle of metal, and a prison tower is really just the same. With essences revealed, it becomes easier to see the connection between unlike things. I believe this practice makes us better at seeing what we all, as human beings, share in common as well. It's all part of the work of getting to radiance, work made easier by not having too many things in the way.

Larissa Kokernot as Molly Brown on brass bed, *The Unsinkable Molly Brown*, **Hubbs Center for Lifelong Learning, 1999.**

EVERYBODY NEEDS TO SING—AMERICAN MUSICALS
Fairy Tale Group #3

THE WAY AMERICAN MUSICALS are usually presented—in big theaters with elaborate and extremely expensive production values—has not appealed to me for most of my adult life. I feel so far away from the emotions onstage, in large part because the acting so often feels shallow and superficial, part of a big production machine that can't slow down for much real truth. In the first few years of Ten Thousand Things, I couldn't imagine us ever doing a musical. I wondered how our audiences would deal with actors suddenly bursting into song using big booming Broadway-style voices, so often seeming intended to show off the singer rather than to help tell the story.

As we continued to tour the plays of Brecht, we couldn't help but notice how the fairly unobtrusive songs in his stories created a powerful attraction. People often gathered with great curiosity around Peter Vitale, our sound maker, wanting to touch the instruments. And whenever a character eased into a song, the audience leaned forward, their attention focused even more keenly on what was happening onstage.

So, despite my reservations, we decided to try a musical, even though we'd only have a one-man orchestra and a cast of no more than eight. I started to think that there was a way that a musical, if set in another time and place, could be a kind of fairy tale, too. I felt there must be a way to get at the essence of a musical, strip it down to its fundamental story line, and truly explore the complexities of the situations through good acting. Peter was a huge fan of the genre and brought me a tall stack of scripts and CDs. I read them all, but when I excitedly brought Peter my choice, the story that had tugged at me the most, he was horrified. In my overall musical ignorance, focusing only on the stories and text, out of the stack of classics I had chosen the one Peter, musically at least, detested.

THE UNSINKABLE MOLLY BROWN   *The Unsinkable Molly Brown*, though based on the true story of a young woman born into poverty who ends up striking it rich, is a fairy tale. Living in another time and another place, Colorado in the late 1800s, Molly, with a cyclone of desires swirling inside her, sets off into the world to try to satisfy her enormous appetites. As she leaves her family's little Colorado mining shack, her father asks her, "What would be enough, Molly?" Molly doesn't really know—she has an endless list—but she answers very honestly, "I ain't settlin' for happiness."

Molly ends up getting hired at a saloon and falling in love with a poor young miner, Johnny Brown. But she makes it very clear from the start that love isn't enough—Johnny needs to be rich before she'll marry him. Luckily, Johnny soon strikes gold, and Molly quickly becomes one of the wealthiest women in the land, living in a mansion in Denver, traveling to Paris to meet painters and poets. Johnny Brown, though, is not comfortable with wealth and is made unhappy by their lavish lifestyle. Molly finds herself having to choose between his deep love and her fabulous riches.

Molly doesn't back away from her fortune. As she tells her father at the beginning of the play, "It ain't the money I love, Pa. It's the not having it I hate." The story actually seemed a fun but important exploration of that age-old question of love or money, a question that we in the middle and upper classes answer all too easily, spouting back with truisms, "Why, love is all you need, of course!" Molly, born into poverty, seemed to be taking a much more honest look at that question, and I sensed that our nontraditional audiences, living with the reality of not having enough money, would also give more weight to the difficulty of the choice. I relished the chance to explore it all with them.

For Johnny Brown, love truly is enough. "You're all I want in this life," he says to Molly, purely and simply, and he actually means it. With his character, I wanted to take a hard look at how challenging that would really be. At one point, Johnny sings a song to Molly, "I'll Never Say No to You." When I was reading the script, I considered this not as a "song" but as text the character was speaking; I marveled at the difficulty involved in really meaning those words. To never say no? The fact that a male character was truly committing to such words made it all the more interesting. It would take enormous trust and enormous discipline; it would be so impossibly hard not to say no at least sometimes to the requests of the one you loved. But Johnny really did seem to be one of those rare men who is willing to accept a woman with all her complexities and difficulties. After giving Molly all the mansions and gowns and jewels and parties that she had asked for, Johnny says to her quietly, "You don't know what it is you do want. But I guess you gotta keep looking." Such acceptance of another person's true and very different self was quite moving.

And the miracle of this rare acceptance finally gets through to Molly, too, though almost too late. Johnny, drowning in the unhappiness of all their material wealth, does finally have to say no to one of Molly's desires: her request for a divorce. He can't allow it, but he lets her go back to Paris, the place where she had felt so happy, amusing the nobility there. Once back in Europe, Molly takes off her wedding ring and discovers an inscription on the inside that Johnny made long ago, "Always remember I love you—and the name of the bank." This honest acknowledgment of the truth of who Molly really is, someone who will always need both love *and* money, is what makes her go rushing back across the sea, into Johnny's arms. So at the play's ending, Molly again has both wealth and love in abundance in her life—and we are still not sure which is more important. Money or love. I loved the honesty of this "fairy tale" ending, a very happy one, but with its big question still intact.

The Unsinkable Molly Brown wasn't just a play, of course; it was a musical. Peter's dislike of the play was due entirely to the music, which he felt was at best unmemorable and at worst mind-numbingly simple. I hadn't listened to the CD; I'd only read the story. And of course *Molly Brown* had scenes in mansions in Denver and palaces in Paris, with ball gowns and jewels and fancy furniture; it seemed like it was going to need a lot of *things*. We couldn't, of course, have an orchestra, just Peter's one-man band. But I had also never seen the movie with Debbie Reynolds, and my ignorance was once again an asset. I clung to my conviction that as long as the story was really interesting and compelling, inviting everyone in, we could make it work. Even though, as usual, we started out not knowing how exactly to do that.

I did know that, as always, we would need excellent actors to bring out the truths and complexities of the story. I'd need an exceptionally special actor to play Johnny, one who could give body to the truth of the difficult work required to "never say no." I needed someone who already knew about the discipline and patience behind such love. At auditions, a tall, lanky actor finally came into the room, radiating a kind of quiet white light, and I knew at once that we had found our Johnny. The only problem, as Peter patiently pointed out, was that he couldn't sing. Well, he could sing a little, I countered; his quavering voice could actually hit *most* of the required notes. Peter, demonstrating a kind of Johnny Brown–like patience and trust himself, sighed and said he would try to make it work.

Not only was I doing a play with music Peter didn't like, I wasn't approaching any of it as he thought it should be approached. Peter, in addition to being an actor, was formally trained in voice for opera as well as musical theater and could play an astonishing array of instruments. But Peter was also a very kind man and a very good listener. He had worked with Ten Thousand Things' nontraditional audiences enough to know that they would probably be quite skeptical of, and even resistant to, a character who just burst into big, full-voiced song. He shared with me an interest in discovering just why—and how—a character would start to sing, knowing that the transition would have to be made in a clear and sensible way. I wanted to pare everything way back, strip it all down so we could see what was going on. Every person at some time in their lives, even if only as a child, has felt the need to burst spontaneously into song. The impulse often gets beaten out of us fairly early on, and as adults most of us rarely indulge it. If our audiences were going to buy that this could really happen, the transitions would be the key. Our actors would really have to earn their right to sing, each and every time. We would have to thoroughly explore every transition.

If I could have had my way, I would have had all the characters sing everything *a cappella*. I wanted to hear all the nuances of the honesty and vulner-

ALL THE LIGHTS ON

ability and complexity while they sang. I didn't want any of it covered up by other instruments, and *a cappella* would make the transition into the song clearest and most transparent. But Peter recognized what a disaster that could be for untrained singers and found ways to gently and sparely support the actors with a guitar strum or a few plunked notes on a toy piano. He was brilliant at pulling sounds out of the actual environment to become musical accompaniment. He helped me, who only knew how to think theatrically, not musically, find a way to get at the musical truth of the story.

And as for all the fancy sets and props this musical about becoming rich seemed to require, we again found that stripping away and paring down brought both great pleasure and truth. Toy furniture would do the trick. The richer Molly got, the smaller her furniture would become: the piano in the saloon where Molly first stopped on her journey was toddler sized, perhaps three or four feet high; the one in Mrs. McGloin's Denver mansion was only about eight inches tall (though still playable—we made a splurge purchase from the American Girl doll catalog). Always aware of the limitations in sight lines that come with no risers, we raised the little piano and other toy red velvet furniture up, mounting it on poles at the actors' eye level so that audience members seated two or three rows back in the circle could see. For the surprise of a curtain rising to show the new Denver digs, we wheeled in the pole tops covered with pieces of cloth, and Molly unveiled each little piece of furniture as the scene began. Finally, in her Paris apartment, Molly unveiled the objects on the poles to reveal, to the approval of her high-society guests, tiny gold velvet doll house sofas and chairs, just a few inches tall; there was great hilarity to be had at the seriousness with which the nobility handled the teeny, thimble-size champagne glasses and rested their fingers on the little divans, the smallness heightening the silliness of all the elaborate material display.

For costumes, we again created a universe of fabric. This time the characters shared coarse woven browns for the Colorado mining world, with a few hints of red in smoother, shinier cloth, bringing in more fancy red fabric as Molly scaled society's heights. We brought in shiny golds when Molly reached Paris—but never completely covered the coarse brown cloth underneath. Something about the form of the musical caused us to become a little extravagant; our designer, the multitalented actress Signe Albertson, had great fun making elaborate and ridiculous hats for the high-society folks.

As exciting as we felt all our theatrical choices to be, the ultimate moment of truth in any Ten Thousand Things show comes when we step in front of the audience. I experienced one of my strongest "you must be out of your mind" moments ever on this tour, standing at the back of the men's prison gym, watching the guys file in. I was doing *The Unsinkable Molly Brown?* For male inmates? What in God's name was I thinking? Experience had taught me that men were usually not that interested in stories about women. They were generally not fans of musicals. And yet. Molly had started out poor and rough and tumble, just as most of them had, though her Rocky Mountain shack provided welcome imaginative distance from the urban poverty many knew so well. As she wrestled with her brothers in the Colorado dirt, she shouted out the words to a song:

There'll come a time cause
Nothin [slam] ner
Nobody wants me
Down like I wants me up [slam]
Up where the people are
Up where the talking is
Up where the joke's goin
On! Now look-a here
I am important to
Me [slam] I ain't no
Bottom to no pile!

I could feel the men start to open up. They were rooting for Molly. They didn't even seem to think her anthem "I'm gonna learn to read and write" was corny. They seemed to accept the ferocity of her desires wholeheartedly.

This story was also very much about class, for Molly, despite all the gold that Johnny had found, never really fit in with the old money wealth. Her generosity and honesty were just too much for the society people of Denver to handle. Molly never took her wealth for granted or felt that it should be used as a way to exclude others. "Already took ten million outta God's good earth. Guess he deserves a little kickback," she exclaimed as she wrote a ridiculously generous check to a Denver priest trying to raise funds for charity. The male inmates took to Molly's out-of-place honesty so much that by the end of the play they were standing and chanting "Mol-ly! Mol-ly!" during curtain call. We were stunned. Another monumental failure on our part to imagine the audience. We could not have dreamed that these men would care so much about a musical about a girl.

I hadn't had any doubt that the female inmates would love Molly. This was one of the first shows we did in both men and women's prisons, and it was truly fascinating to see how starkly different the reactions were at some parts of the story. The musical is certainly about class and wealth, but it's also about romance and sex, and each gender brought a very different perspective to those scenes. For many women, Johnny's undying love for Molly touched a powerful chord, reminding them of their own lonely aches and the absence of sweetness and tenderness in their lives. Many of the women sobbed openly, at times so hard that one or two needed to run across the stage into the bathroom to get tissue.

Then there was the "gift-giving scene." Johnny, having just struck the vein of gold, returns to their little mountain cabin to present Molly with a series of presents. He unveils several toddler-size pieces of furniture, including a new wood-burning stove (made from a trash can we'd turned over and painted black). He then comes to the final brown cloth and pulls it off to reveal a toddler-size brass bed, entwined with roses about its frame. The women burst into ooohs and ahhs, so touched at the loveliness and thoughtfulness of the gift.

The men's reaction to the unveiling of the brass bed was quite different. When the brown cloth was pulled off, they burst into loud whoops and hollers of delight. To their way of thinking, Molly had just received a bunch of presents from Johnny, and now it was her turn to give some payback. The brass bed meant only one thing to this audience—sex. The actor playing Johnny Brown, Ron Menzel, however, seized on the men's honesty as a chance to have a "conversation" with them. As an actor, he felt able to harness their energies

Molly and Johnny's happy ending in front of their Lincoln Log palace, Hubbs Center for Lifelong Learning, 1999.

by using his next lines like a lasso, pulling them away from the idea of sex and guiding them over toward still more romance. When Molly exclaimed at his gift, "You got yourself a bed, I'll say that for you, Leadville," Johnny gave his next lines a stronger than usual subtext. Underneath his actual words to Molly, "Yeah, and at night the moon comes a-shinin' in and it's all starry like," Ron was also saying to the men, "No guys, we're not going to demand sex now, we're gonna give her still more, we're going to recite her a sonnet. Giving, without asking for anything in return. That's what love is." The men's surprise was visceral. Though some resisted, making disdainful sneers, you could actually feel most of the others deciding to go along with Johnny to see what would happen. When an audience is so open and honest, true conversations can happen during the performance without any change to the actual lines of the script.

Molly Brown brought us another of our most radiant performance moments, this time again at the Dorothy Day Center for the homeless in downtown St. Paul. For a while when I was contemplating doing the play, I worried about its "happy ending." Perhaps the story was too much of a fairy tale. People in our audiences clearly knew that life almost never ended up like Molly's, leaping from poverty to enormous wealth, and I didn't want anyone to think that we were suggesting this was easy or even remotely possible. But *Molly Brown* wasn't a typical American rags-to-riches story, either. Molly and Johnny didn't end up with what they had through hard work—Johnny discovered that vein of gold through sheer luck. Both characters are always very clear about this. And truth be told, I thought, we would all be better off if wealthy people were so honest. So many end up with their money through accidents of geography or birth, with strokes of good timing, fortuitous connections, and the help of others all playing much more important roles than any one individual's effort. Luck has so much to do with why some people get rich and others don't. It's a relief to be reminded of this sometimes. And with Molly's journey, because there had been so much laughter and delight and silliness along the way, it became clear, after several performances, that our audiences wanted it to end well for her, wishing the same good fortune for themselves.

But even I could not bring myself to end the play with everyone singing one more round of Molly's anthem, "I'm gonna learn to read and write." The reprise seemed tired and trivial by that point. At the time, the pop group Barenaked Ladies was quite popular, and in rehearsal someone started singing their song, "If I Had a Million Dollars." It became instantly clear to all of us that this was the perfect song to end with. As we drew near the end of our performance at the Dorothy Day Center, Molly and Johnny started to waltz in front of their little log cabin—now fancier with additions (we'd built one out of Lincoln logs and put it up on a pole); the rest of the cast started to sing, "If I had a million dollars, I would buy you a house." A few members of the audience started to chime in. It seemed a lot of homeless people were quite tuned in to popular culture. Soon, almost everyone in the very large room was singing, "If I had a million dollars, we wouldn't have to eat Kraft dinner (but we would eat Kraft dinner, of course we would, we'd just eat more) . . . If I had a million dollars, I'd buy you a monkey (haven't you always wanted a monkey?)." So much joy and warmth among people, people from all kinds of different economic circumstances, all united for a few moments by acknowledging, with humor and heart, that in our world, both love *and* money—or at least our fantasies about what money can buy—bring enormous pleasure.

THE MOST HAPPY FELLA   After *The Unsinkable Molly Brown*, we all decided we loved doing musicals. Musicals just made everyone happy, from the artists who worked on them in fun, music-filled rehearsal processes to the audiences who experienced them. Working within the necessary strictures of Ten Thousand Things performance conditions and our need to imagine a first-time audience's reception of people who suddenly burst into song actually just made it all even more fun. We next turned to *The Most Happy Fella*, the story about the unlikely romance between the elderly Napa Valley vineyard owner Tony and the young waitress Rosabella. The idea of an unlikely love match was often echoed in the actual performance itself, particularly one very memorable show at a men's prison, all through the medium of one very implausible and reimagined song.

In addition to the tricky romance of Rosabella and Tony, the musical offers several other unusual love matches, including one between Herman, a sweet, shy ranch hand, and Cleo, another waitress, but a brash, outspoken one from Texas. We had the enormous good fortune to be able to cast a former Minnesota Vikings noseguard in the role of Herman. Esera Tuaolo is of Samoan descent, and as his former job description suggests, he is an enormous, powerfully muscular man, but one whose inner being perfectly matches Herman's sweetness and kindness. And he can sing with all his soul.

There is a moment near the end of the play where Cleo gets in a fight and is roughly handled by another ranch hand. Herman's protective instincts spring into action, and, completely out of character, he punches the accoster. He is so surprised by this action that he finds he has to sing. In the original 1950s version, Herman's song, "I Made a Fist," is a triumphant celebration of his masculinity, complete with marching brass band. Peter and I knew we could never go into a men's prison—a place where so many found themselves trapped because of acts of violence—and sing such a song. But once again, our necessarily spare approach to the material came to the rescue. Peter noticed that when the brass band accompaniment was stripped away, the melody of "I Made a Fist" was actually somewhat melancholy. Esera began the song very quietly, with only one spare piano note as accompaniment, and the song became not a celebration but a sad realization of his discovery of his ability to hurt people.

When we first walked into the men's prison gym, many of the guys quickly recognized Esera from his Vikings days and gathered around to admire the tattoos on his astonishing biceps as we set up. At this time, the prison would not allow chairs in the gym, for fear they might scratch the floor, so the men sat on mats that ringed the playing space. When Esera began to sing his first song, "I Like Everybody That I've Ever Met," tossing in a little dancing as well, you could clearly see the shock on most of the men's faces. This astonishment transformed into a sort of open-jawed wonder as the story exerted its pull and the men, seemingly without realizing it, dropped their defenses and entered the fairy tale world with the requisite naïveté.

I especially loved how this primarily African American male audience (an enraging reality of male incarceration, but that's for another book) seemed to completely empathize with the plight of vineyard owner Tony, who was quite

Esera Tuaolo as
Herman in *The
Most Happy Fella*,
2001.

tall, thin, elderly, and very white. But Tony was also an immigrant, an outsider who couldn't speak English well and who felt ashamed of himself. Tony's vulnerability about these shortcomings provided the men a strong connection to the character, so that neither his wealth nor his skin color got in the way.

By the time Herman got to singing about the punch he had just thrown, the men had opened up completely. As Esera sang about the pain of discovering that as a large strong man, he had the power to hurt others, I looked around the circle of audience and saw tears glimmering in many of the men's eyes. Men in prison usually need to be cautious and guarded, but this was one of the most open men's prison audiences I have ever experienced. The Broadway musical of the 1950s had met with the Minnesota Vikings and inmates in a men's prison through the artists of Ten Thousand Things. Our spare reimagining of a story—and an unlikely romance between all these partners—blossomed in that prison's gym.

Reimagining the stories of musicals through the eyes of our nontraditional audiences has also served to delight our veteran theater audiences, who take great pleasure in the way the stories are refreshed. We can explore what happens to *My Fair Lady* if Eliza Doolittle, not Henry Higgins, truly becomes the center of the story; or what happens to *Ragtime* if there are only eight actors, plus a few puppets and props to tell the epic historic tale; or what happens to *Man of La Mancha* if the whole story, which is told by inmates in a prison, actually only uses the objects that can fit in Cervantes's battered trunk. In all of these, the stakes become very high, the situations have new urgency, the lower-income characters receive much more attention, and the humanity of the stories shines even more brightly when all the glitz is stripped away. This seems to delight experienced and perhaps somewhat jaded audiences who have seen many productions of the same shows before.

CAROUSEL Once in a while, our traditional audiences have been unable to put aside their own expectations of what a musical should be. I was attracted to Rodgers and Hammerstein's *Carousel* as a story about working-class people. The characters were all trying to scrape through a hardscrabble existence, working in factories and fishing on rough seas. But it was all still approachable

Regina Williams as Aldonza, *Man of La Mancha*, women's correctional facility, 2011.

as a fairy tale because of its setting in an unfamiliar time and place. Peter had wanted to do this musical for a long time, but I had resisted because I found the misogyny so relentless. I finally saw a way in, though, when I thought of casting a particular actress, Carolyn Goelzer, as Julie. Julie would need to be tough, to stand up as fiercely as she could to the misogynistic forces around her. Carolyn was large and strong, with a deep raspy voice, and, although very attractive in her strength, not conventionally so, certainly nothing like Shirley Jones in the movie. The actor playing Billy Bigelow, Terry Hempleman, was not the most accomplished singer, but he also brought a knowledge of working-class life in his very being that lent great credibility to the story.

In the men's prison, overcome with a need to sing about his love, Billy's rendition of "If I Loved You" was tentative and awkward; he was not a man who was used to singing. The inmates seemed not only to accept this but to welcome it. Billy was singing like they would sing if they ever had to. Precisely because of Billy's untrained voice, the men were able to accept the strangeness of the musical form. After that particular performance, all of us in the cast and crew were quite moved and inspired by the connections the story had made with the inmates. But our traditional audiences just did not seem to be able to shake John Raitt and his big booming operatic voice from their minds, nor to let go of their idea that Julie should be petite and pretty. Though female inmates had screamed with laughter at the antics of the shifty-eyed Jigger, even chanting his name every time he appeared, our paying audiences did not find him funny at all. It was probably our most schizophrenic tour, in terms of the completely different responses of traditional and nontraditional audiences.

MY FAIR LADY   We are sometimes able to cast excellent actors who are also fantastic singers, though acting excellence is always the first requirement. With *My Fair Lady*, guest directed by Lear deBessonet, we were excited to work with one of the best singers in town, a wonderful, kind, generous man who was also an amazing actor, blessed with great comic physical and improvisatory skills. In addition to playing the housekeeper Mrs. Pearce, Bradley Greenwald played the part of Freddy, the young upper-class man who becomes smitten with Eliza. This meant he got to sing "On the Street Where You Live" with his beautiful, classically trained tenor voice, a moment which always brought all of us in the cast, and in our paying audiences, to tears. In the prisons, not so much. As soon as his voice started to boom out, large and full, we could sense a barrier of suspicion go up among the audience. Music from different cultures often has politics attached to it—not every kind of music is equally appealing to everyone, and musical theater music is no exception. Because Bradley was such a wonderful actor and able to sing with such sincerity and heart, he eventually won the nontraditional audiences over—but it wasn't an easy victory. It often took until almost the end of the song for audiences unfamiliar with the form to get over their suspicions and work around the initial obstacle that Bradley's well-trained voice presented. With Ten Thousand Things, we have to find an approachable, egalitarian playing field for musical styles, too, inviting everyone in as best we can, whether it's an invitation to nontraditional audiences to enter a Broadway show tune or one to our older, whiter traditional audiences to try out some hip-hop, as with Will Power's *The Seven*.

We now do a musical almost every season. They make us happy, and their fairy tale qualities, in addition to their songs, really do deeply engage our audience. I don't think our approach to the musical is unique. Many other theaters, especially in recent years, have discovered the joys and blessings of doing musicals in a pared-down style. But at Ten Thousand Things it's all out of necessity. In our fifteen-foot performance space, three people can easily make a chorus; a dance is just several people moving to music together, usually in a very pedestrian way. But it all has an enormous impact because the audience is so close. The necessity of imagining the lives of very different audiences gives us fresh perspective.

When you've never seen live theater before, let alone a musical, it is truly bizarre when people just start to sing in the middle of a scene. Many in our audiences have suspicions about musicals to begin with, just as I did. But because we are always trying to be honest about the need to sing, not trying to impress with how good the voices are, these people can enter the world of musicals, too. They can connect because once in a while they too have felt the need to sing, in the shower or perhaps even while walking down the street, when no one else is around. It's a simple human urge.

Several years after *The Unsinkable Molly Brown* tour, I was walking down the hall of that same men's prison where we first opened, preparing to do another play. The hall was empty at the time, except for an approaching inmate. I was a little nervous, but as he came nearer, I could tell he was singing. He was singing "Belly Up to the Bar, Boys." He gave me a big grin and waved as we passed. Not only had a musical connected with an unlikely audience in the moment—it had stayed around for quite a long time.

A Midsummer Night's Dream cast in pajamas at curtain call, Avalon School, 2013.

CONCEPT-FREE DIRECTING— ORIGINALITY FROM NECESSITY
Preparation, Rehearsals

AS A DIRECTOR, I never worry about how to make my work "original." In the Twin Cities, theater audiences might choose between a Shakespeare comedy set in the Roaring Twenties and one set on a cruise ship; the Ten Thousand Things version of the play will be focused on telling the story with as much clarity and as few objects as possible. I do want freshness and originality to be abundant in the production, but this just happens out of necessity, without any conscious effort to "come up with a concept." If I just do what I have to, viewing the story through the eyes of all our different audiences and solving problems within our bare-bones performance constraints, then a truly unique perspective, full of all kinds of interesting and unusual choices, emerges quite naturally, without my really having to try.

At the moment, I'm working on *A Midsummer Night's Dream*. I'll use it as an example to go through my working process, some of which is probably not so different from what many directors do. Although *Midsummer* is most certainly a fairy tale in the true sense of the word, I resisted it for a long time. The productions I had seen, often in school or community theater settings, had been so annoying, with most characters presented superficially for cheap laughs. It didn't feel like anything crucial was at stake, beyond some mixed-up love matches. But the working-class characters known as the Rude Mechanicals broadened the world of the play to include people who weren't just of the nobility. And it certainly was set in another time and place.

As often happens, the prison audiences leapt to the forefront of my imaginings; this time it was the men. With their misogyny often openly and honestly expressed, in my imagination male inmates can present the most formidable resistance to entering a lot of plays, resistance for me to try to figure out how to overcome. My instincts immediately told me that we would need to use Shakespeare's term "goblin" much more often than "fairy," as the guys in prison would most likely not be too enthused about delicate gauzy sprites with gossamer wings. Okay, we could have goblins.

I read the script again, and as I did, I felt that intuitive tug, the pull that told me something important was going on in the story that might be of vital interest to all our audiences. I found myself being drawn to one aspect of the behavior of the indistinguishable lovers, Helena, Hermia, Lysander, and Demetrius—their extreme shifts between complete love for and absolute hatred of each other. Those sudden changes in passion would probably resonate. Everyone has been through violent, horrible breakups, discovering they suddenly despise the person they once intensely desired. I decided to plunge in and keep trying to figure out just what was going on.

EIGHT ACTORS But first, I put aside the search to find the play's common struggle, one shared by all the characters (and the audience as well, of course), and turned, as I often do, to thinking about the practical issues involved in staging it, just to make sure it was feasible. Thinking through the necessities of our performance constraints often helps me shed light on the heart of the play. There were over twenty roles, so how many actors would we need? Eight is usually the maximum number I cast in a large play. Double- and even triple-casting is a necessity for us, in part because of the budgetary benefits, but even more because such casting ensures that everyone will be able to be onstage as much as possible, something both actors and audiences enjoy. Very large casts, in which some actors have only one small part with a few lines and spend a great deal of time sitting around waiting to go on, often feel sluggish, both in rehearsals and in performances, where audiences sense how little of the actors' energies are being used. Most actors, at least the kind of generous, playful actors I like to work with, are happiest when they're onstage a lot, and audiences quickly pick up on the fun they're having.

Midsummer has three groups of characters: the nobility, the workers, and

ALL THE LIGHTS ON

the goblins. I started to make charts of the scenes. If each actor played one character in each of those three groups, it might work. It would mean some lightning-fast costume changes, though, so the costumes would have to be really simple, with one well-defined piece for each character. I reasoned that there would need to be a base costume that the other pieces could be thrown over. Pajamas popped to mind. It's a midsummer night's *dream*, after all. The pajamas could all be different shapes and textures, so it wouldn't be boring to look at, but if they all shared the same color, some sort of dark midnight blue, with maybe some flashes of silvery gray, those colors could help create a world of the night sky, of the darkness and mystery of the forest. I also liked how having that base costume equalized all three groups of characters, so you couldn't say which was more important—the nobles, the workers, or the goblins. You also couldn't really tell which was the most "real." The actors in pajamas were really dreamers, stepping into different lives for a little bit, as we all do when we dream, when we watch a play—or when we empathize with someone who is different.

MISOGYNY ONCE AGAIN   It's not unusual for me to be irritated by at least some parts of almost every play I choose to work on; irritation can serve as an irresistible challenge to figure out how to overcome. One of my major sources of irritation with *A Midsummer Night's Dream* is, of course, its overwhelming sexism. Once again, even as I loved the bigness of the world of this classical play, I was immediately wearied by the narrow treatment of its few female characters. How could anyone believe that Hippolyta, the Amazon queen whom Theseus had captured and was now forcing into marriage, could ever become a willing partner to such a wedding? And this play had the old tired drama around a father, Egeus, forcing a daughter, Hermia, to marry someone she doesn't want to. This kind of conflict has so little relevance today, at least in most Western cultures. I was bored by it. In the goblin world we had the cruelty of Oberon, tricking and even drugging his queen, Titania, so she would give up the child of a dear friend who had died in childbirth, a child she had promised to raise as her own. I was just really tired of all these situations, and I had no idea how anyone could view them as palatable, let alone enjoyable, as most of the other mind-numbing productions I had seen had asked me to do.

CASTING These irritations immediately caused me once again to turn my attention to casting as one way to ease some of my annoyance. There is that old directing school adage that "casting is 90 percent of directing." I actually believe this to be fairly true. But it doesn't seem that most directors put 90 percent of their creative energies into casting. I've heard of other directors placing a lot of energy into finding the right "type" for a part. But viewing actors and characters as "types" does not seem to me to require much creativity.

For me, casting is where my creativity truly begins. It stems from the simple notion that because I know that every kind of human will be in my audience, I need to find room in the play for as many kinds of humans as possible, putting as many races, ages, shapes, and sizes onstage as I can. These are wonderful colors and textures to paint any story with. I don't call this color-"blind" casting, of course, because great attention and care must be paid to the way actors of color are used, especially taking into consideration the history of oppression, discrimination, and hurtful portrayals each race and gender has had to bear. I especially, as you know by now, want to find room for women, who always make up more than half my audience, with some audiences entirely female. Thus, if at all possible, I want women to have at least 50 percent of the space in any story we tell. Smart, imaginative casting can so easily bring fresh perspectives and new insights to any play. It is astonishing to me how much fun it is to do—but how few directors really do it.

Perhaps the general lack of creativity on the part of directors when they cast is partly because many contemporary plays seem too "realistic" for creative casting. But I believe that need not always be the case. *A Streetcar Named Desire*, for example, at first seems not to be a good fit for Ten Thousand Things, in part because it is confined to a small, naturalistic 1940s New Orleans apartment with all white characters. But the story of family dysfunction was compelling and universal. We just needed to find a way to open up the world to more of our audiences. We did cast a white man as Stanley, but we also cast an African American woman as Blanche, a Dominican American woman as

Stella, and an Asian American man as Mitch. It was completely believable. New Orleans has always been a place of great diversity. More important, the casting invited our audience into the story in a way that an all-white cast simply could not have done. I like to call this color-*ful* casting, casting actors of all colors with great thought and care. Or, even better, "creative" casting, as opposed to standard, unimaginative "typecasting," which can actually feed into stereotyping.

I am actually very rarely interested in plays that "require" me to cast by type. Plays that demand a very specific age and look, a thirty-year-old woman with blonde hair, slim waist, and attractive appearance, for example, are usually not fairy tales. They almost always leave lots of people out. I also don't like plays with such instructions because they limit my creativity as a director. In fact, these days, when I see that a play has an all-white cast my immediate response is to feel much less interested in attending. Not only do such plays leave others out; they are usually blissfully unaware that they are doing so. I find it wearying and sometimes even painful to sit in their audiences.

Of course, you can't cast just anyone as anything. Each role does have certain contours and confines that a director needs to come to understand. But if a play does seem to demand that someone of a specific race or gender be cast in a part, then I want to take a hard look at why this should be. Sometimes it's just the demands of a heterosexual romance, but there will often be racism or sexism involved. I love to challenge myself to think as expansively about those demands as I can, which can be a great deal of fun.

Returning to *Midsummer*, clear about the need for each actor to play two or three parts, I started looking for more roles for women. A woman could be Puck, of course; there's nothing unusual in that idea, and I realized a woman could also easily play Bottom. All the Rude Mechanicals could be women, really. Indeed, when the usually all-male Rude Mechanicals put on their play, they cast Flute as a woman in the role of Thisbe. So we could certainly do some gender stretching, too. But if each Mechanical also had to be a member of the nobility, how could we do all the romances? Well, there actually isn't any reason why one of the romances couldn't be between two women. Lysander could be a woman, easily. I couldn't imagine much resistance to such a same-sex match up among the female inmates, or among the male inmates either, for that matter (a male couple, we'd learned from *The Seven*, was more challenging for the men). And Egeus could be a dominating mother, rather than a father trying to control a daughter's marriage—that might freshen up that story a bit. Actually, we could probably do the whole play with only two men: one to play King Theseus, and one to play Demetrius in the confusing foursome of noble lovers. I started to imagine what other roles I might cast these two men in.

In dreams and in plays, we can escape the confines of our gender. What if King Theseus, in a dream of the goblin world, found himself having to be Titania, the goblin Queen? And the captive Amazon Queen Hippolyta might dream herself to be the goblin King, Oberon? That would help address some of the gender imbalance. And of course the actor playing Demetrius, when he entered the Rude Mechanical world, would have to be Flute, the one that gets cast as a woman in the play that the workers put on. What fun!

It's all about opening things up. This is actually the biggest reason I love to throw so much of my creative energies into casting. Creative casting opens up possibilities for audiences that have often felt trapped by the perceptions of others. Such casting opens up exciting new possibilities for actors, too, who are so often boxed in and shut down as they are cast over and over again by type. It allows them instead to stretch their muscles with many varied characters. It lets audiences take pleasure in how one actor can become so many different people, and thus illuminates the humanity common to all of those characters, whether upper or lower class, male or female. Opening up possibilities means that new energy and radiance is released, both in rehearsals and in performance. There is so much joy and delight in being able to escape from the box, to see and be seen in new light.

Considering the possibilities of casting opened up more depths of the play for me. As the same actors shifted back and forth between the worlds of the nobles, the workers, and the goblins, transforming as we do in our dreams, what if a faint trace of the previous reality sometimes remained? What if King Theseus, suddenly finding himself a fairy Queen, had to experience what it felt like to be dominated by a powerful husband, tricked into doing things he didn't really want to do? What if the captive Amazon Queen Hippolyta suddenly found herself powerful again as a goblin King? Would she experience such power differently, with perhaps some faint memory, as from a dream, of once having been captured? With each actor taking part in all three of *Midsummer*'s worlds, would there be moments when the dreamlike traces of one world might intrude on another? I had no idea, but it seemed like such an interesting idea to explore.

And thus, by thinking about the necessities of casting—and costuming—the terrain of the play was now illuminated for me. I returned to the source of my initial tug about what the common struggle might be, pointed to by the lovers' sudden changes of heart. The leap from loving to hating someone is an extreme shift of reality, one baffling and difficult for anyone to explain. I started to think about how so often in life our realities shift without our even noticing it, except for those few moments when we "wake up" to marvel at the change and wonder how it could have happened. I imagined a woman one day waking up to find herself in a jail cell, having no idea how it had happened. I imagined a man suddenly waking up to find himself living on the streets, wondering just how he had come to be there. A woman looking up from her desk to suddenly notice she had just spent years of her life in a little office in a big law firm, married to a man she was no longer interested in, the mother of resentful, rebellious teenagers, having no idea how such creatures had come to live with her. I began to notice the sudden shifts of reality that most of the characters in *Midsummer* find themselves experiencing, whether from a loving to a hateful relationship, from being a queen to a captive, from being a worker to the lover of a fairy queen.

SLEEPING WHILE STANDING   The characters in *Midsummer* fall asleep onstage a lot. Thinking practically again, I knew anyone lying down on the floor would be a problem because of sight lines. At Ten Thousand Things only people seated in the first row can see what's happening on the ground. (And, it should be noted, the floors at some facilities don't make for pleasant—or sanitary—reclining.) The characters were just going to have to fall asleep standing up. Suddenly, I saw a way the costume changes, the transitions between one world of characters and the next, could work to illuminate the central experience of the play. Sleepwalking. We all sleepwalk through much of our lives, most of us waking up only occasionally to be astonished at how things have changed without our understanding how or why.

If this were a world where people fell asleep standing up, it would be an easy transition to start walking while still sleeping. The pajama-clad actors could do so through the changes, smoothly dropping one costume piece and putting on the next without even being aware. Later in the next scene, we might find a moment where one or two of the actors could briefly "wake up"; they could have a sharp sudden sense that things had been different not too long ago. It would be momentarily bewildering, but then they would just have to carry on with the scene. I knew that too many moments of bewildered walking around could get tedious, but a few moments of recognition of the mysterious shifts would underline all the other places in the play where the characters are suddenly astonished by what seems to have just happened.

As a director, I have certain emotional terrains that I especially love. *Midsummer* would allow me to explore one of my favorites—bewilderment. Those times when we must drop all our pretenses and acknowledge that we are confused and overwhelmed, that we really do not understand at all what is going on. Bewilderment is a great leveler; it is a state of mind all humans—all classes, races, and genders—experience. At bottom, none of us really understands what is going on. I have noticed that when we can acknowledge this together, usually through laughter, when we can admit together publicly that we're really all just pretending to understand, it can be a great source of connection.

Bewilderment is also akin to the states of astonishment and wonder, which express the enormous mystery of life. I love to watch these feelings onstage, but I find they are rarely portrayed, especially in naturalistic theater. I'm not sure why, though it is certainly interesting to think about what this says about our world right now. In any case, *Midsummer* is full of moments of bewilderment, astonishment, and wonder, and I wanted to give them time to live and breathe, time for all of us to recognize such feelings together. Suddenly waking up to discover, in bewilderment, that your life has drastically changed is an experience that every audience member could probably relate to. It's a very interesting territory to explore, and as a director it helped me give the play a shape that would help audiences, in turn, to better grasp its complex story.

SCRIPT WORK With this much clearer sense of a central human experience of the play, I then turn to more mundane script work tasks, more of those directing school fundamentals, which I approach with renewed attention because of Ten Thousand Things' audiences. I work, as most directors do, on finding the actions underlying the characters' lines, trying to understand what each is really trying to do to others when they speak, knowing that the ability to feel the visceral actions underneath the fancy words is the way we all, in the audience, best understand what is going on. Finding the actions while still just reading the script is always a guess at best. I know I won't really understand what's going on until we start to rehearse, but I take an initial stab at it.

After searching for the actions of individual characters, I then try to sense the accumulated impact of all those actions to find the spine—the one central action every character is trying to accomplish, in one way or another. Again, finding a spine is basic directing preparation, but it is particularly crucial in the spare and urgent world of Ten Thousand Things performances, where we all need to be able to easily get at the essence of a play. It's another important way to pare down, to get at what is most important and figure out what we might all share. As I worked on *Midsummer*, it became clear that every character, in one way or another, was trying to somehow pull someone else into their vision of love. That seemed like a common human action that most everyone in our audiences could relate to. We've all struggled with ways to try to make others love us back as much as we love them. It's what each of the lovers is trying to do, of course, as they try to pull each other into marriage. It's what each of the Rude Mechanicals wants to do as they try to make a moving play into which they can pull the lords and ladies in their audience. And it's what the goblins are trying to do as they apply their herbs and drugs and pull their unsuspecting partners into their forced visions.

Some characters are more successful at this than others. I always like to put all the characters on a spectrum to help me understand a play's different points of view. Hermia and Lysander (in my version, the lesbian couple) seem the most successful, as they both willingly fall in love and marry each other. The goblin king Oberon is also "successful," though he has to use magic drugs on Titania. Demetrius also has to be drugged to make him want to return to his original love, Helena. Both those couplings are more than a little unsettling. On the least successful side of the spectrum, to me, it wasn't at all clear that Hippolyta would stay willingly in Theseus's fantasy of a love nest if she weren't forced to.

I decided to put the Rude Mechanicals at the more successful end of the spectrum. Though at first glance they don't seem to have been very successful at getting the nobles to enter the world of their play through their vision of the love story of Pyramus and Thisbe, I knew that in our version the audiences would have to be touched and moved. The lords and ladies certainly make a lot of sarcastic comments about the crudeness of the production. But the Rude Mechanicals themselves believe in their characters wholeheartedly, complete with a terrifying lion and a tragic death scene. They have poured so much love and care into their vision—I knew their play would have to have an impact, just like Ten Thousand Things enlists our audiences' imaginations with a minimum of props, using a great deal of heart and spirit to break down the audience's resistance to seeing the world with naïveté. So, yes, in our version, the Rude Mechanicals, though their production might be awful, would have so much heart and spirit that they would be a success.

When every character in the play is trying to pull someone into their own vision of love, whether it's Helena trying to enchant Demetrius or Quince trying to corral her unruly actors into the reality of her script or Titania trying to seduce Bottom, we get to see this one same situation from many points of view. Given the diversity of our audiences' experiences, I always want to look at the central issues of a play from as many angles and perspectives as I can, raising many questions, suggesting many possible answers, so the experience feels sharp and multifaceted. Shakespeare, with his wide swath of characters, is the very best at providing this for us all.

CHARACTER QUESTIONS   One of the other things I do before I get into a rehearsal room, again certainly not at all unusually, is to come up with as many

ALL THE LIGHTS ON

Gavin Lawrence as
Titania and Elise
Langer as Bottom,
*A Midsummer
Night's Dream*,
Avalon School,
2013.

questions as I can about each character. Knowing that many in my audiences will be experiencing theater for the very first time makes me feel comfortable asking very obvious questions. It is crucial not to take anything for granted—because I know that my audiences won't. And such obvious questioning often leads to new discoveries. Holding in mind the breadth and diversity of my audiences causes me to work hard to ask questions about characters to ferret out their complexities. No character can be dismissed as unimportant or one-dimensional. Whether the character is rich or poor, "good guy" or criminal, onstage a lot or hardly at all, each must be seen as fully human, complicated, with both strengths and flaws. I don't try to answer the questions I raise about the characters, or if I do come up with an answer I just let it float, because I always want to give the actors a chance to answer the questions for themselves, always holding open the possibility that they will develop a much more interesting answer than I have.

SET DESIGN   I completed my pre-rehearsal imagining of the world of *Midsummer* by trying to figure out what the set would be, which basically means figuring out the fewest number of set pieces we would need. The pieces would probably be made out of aluminum, which has become our favorite raw material as it is incredibly light and easy to carry. I had been drawn to Titania's description in Act II of the world as a place at the mercy of seasons, seasons which had become chaotic and unruly with storms and floods, leaving the forest rotted and bare. It reminded me so much of the turbulence that global warming is beginning to unleash on our own world. I hadn't seen *Midsummer* sets that reflected her description (though there certainly may have been some). Those I'd seen were usually lush and magical rather than barren and spare. A barren and spare set, of course, felt right to me! As with all Ten Thousand Things sets, the audience would have to make it lush with their own imaginations. This, after all, was what the characters in the play were so often doing when they transformed a seemingly bleak and hopeless "love landscape" with their own surreal visions.

We needed to create, in our little fifteen-foot-square space, a "forest" of some sort, five or six pieces to make a maze in which characters could become confused and lost. I found a photo of some strange metal sculptures that seemed dripping and rotted, as if the metal had hardened when melting. They were unsettling, and mostly black, but glints of silver metal offered a hint of a strange beauty. I offered the photos to our designer Stephen Mohring as inspiration. We could blacken our light and portable aluminum and then polish bits to let silver shine through. A couple of the same "tree trunk" structures would also need to serve as pillars or columns of some sort when we were outside the royal palace. I also wanted a little height in the world, to reflect the play's sense of hierarchy as well as provide relief to the eye. It's funny how someone stepping up even just a few inches can create intense focus. Theseus could stand on a little aluminum step of some kind outside the palace; when moved to another spot onstage, this piece could also serve as a little hillock in the forest and a place for Titania's bower. As I thought about how we would move the hillock around, I realized that the actors could lift it over their heads and carry it across stage, so its circular bottom turned toward the audience could perhaps suggest the crescent moon, which offers only a sliver of light in the dark play. Stephen took in all the requirements and created beautiful and strange objects—narrow, twisted columnar structures from winding strips of aluminum that allowed the audience to see through them, preventing the trunks from being visual obstacles. The hillock was just a skeleton structure, too, with a pounded aluminum crescent moon shape on its bottom.

What was most interesting to me about the bleak world of *Midsummer* was that it was caused by the jealous quarreling of the goblin king and queen. Their wild, impulsive emotions were at the root of all the destruction and chaos. That's what the goblins must be: impulsive, emotional, irrational, and thus often, though not always, destructive. They were the lunatics, I thought, really. Theseus's famous speech dismissing nobles, lunatics, and lovers came to mind. The nobles were the lovers. And the Rude Mechanicals were the poets when they created and performed their play. All three groups dreamed up realities and tried to impose them on others. And all three experienced prolonged moments of bewilderment, moments in between worlds, when they realized that their realities had changed, not really knowing how. Each group really could be said to be lunatics, lovers, and poets, all three at once, and each actor in pajamas would play parts in all three worlds as well.

I write about all this in such detail not because I think my ideas about *Midsummer* are astonishing or brilliant. There have been many deeply original productions of this story. I just wanted to take you through my particular preparation process as a director to help you see how simply imagining all my different audiences as I read, from the skeptical male inmates to the women who make up the majority of my audience (and of almost every theater audience) and who are tired of seeing such limited portrayals of themselves, causes me to reimagine casting. This imagining, in addition to wrestling with the necessary constraints of our spare productions, causes me to fairly effortlessly come up with an approach into the play. The need for the eight actors who have to play all the parts to have a base costume suggests, quite obviously, pajamas. The need for actors to remain standing so that the whole audience can see them means they will have to sleep standing up, which easily leads to sleepwalking between scenes. It's really not much fancier than that. A framework has been uncovered. Now on to see what happens in rehearsals.

REHEARSALS   Rehearsals are for me a sacred space. They are a place for me to practice being the best human being that I can possibly be. They provide a place for me to practice treating others with kindness, generosity, and honesty, creating as much room as possible for playfulness, hilarity, and delight. From the very first day I try to make rehearsals a place where we all feel safe to profess our ignorance, to say "I don't know" and "I don't understand." It must be a place to take risks and make a fool of oneself. These are the conditions that make true discovery possible and that allow the radiance of the actor to begin to shine.

Making rehearsals into a radiant space also includes being respectful of people's time. I try to structure rehearsals so that people have to be there as little as possible. Just as it is an energy drag during performances to have actors sitting around offstage for long periods, the same holds true in rehearsals. Everyone leads such busy lives that if I can release people to attend to other matters when they aren't really needed, I find their attention and focus to be even stronger and clearer when they are present. I try to give out rehearsal schedules a week ahead of time so people can plan around it. We just rehearse five days a week, during the daytime, with weekends off, which not only makes life so much easier for actors with children and families but, I am convinced, also creates a level of relaxation that allows for more "simmering on the back burner" and a deeper creativity than is possible with just one day off a week. I love time off during rehearsals, so I've learned to become efficient at solving problems. Sometimes I even end rehearsal early, having accomplished everything I wanted for the day. This respect for time is returned with gratitude and renewed focus on the part of the actors, making the rehearsal room that much more pleasant and productive.

FIRST DAY   On the first day of rehearsal, we sit in a circle, without a table, open and available to each other without any kind of barrier, and begin by going through a little ritual. Everyone offers a story about a memorable Ten

Thousand Things performance moment. From that very first day, all of us, both veterans and newcomers, are reminded of our priorities. For our work, the audience must be at the center. Not the playwright's intent, not the director's vision, not the actor's brilliant choices. For us, the necessity of connecting with the audience is always the determining factor in our decision making. And this audience is very different from the one taken for granted in other rehearsal spaces. We try to imagine how the story we want to tell will be of interest. On that first day, especially after hearing a few excruciating tales of past shows, it becomes very clear that if the audience isn't engaged, disaster lurks. That prospect is a huge motivator in helping everyone to focus in right away. Fear isn't the only motivator, of course. The exhilarating stories provide the sense that if we can connect this story to our audiences' lives, great reward and satisfaction await. The awareness that we only have bodies, live sounds, and the words of the play with which to tell the story also enters in. The stakes on the first day of rehearsal become very high, and not because anyone is worried about what critics might think.

Next, I offer what I think I've figured out so far about the play, a sort of framework for us to focus in on as we work. For *Midsummer*, I offered much of what I've written about so far in this chapter as our point of departure. This part of the day's schedule gets shorter and shorter the older I get. I've become much more efficient at putting up a framework for our play. Then it's time to let my preparatory work go and see what the other talented people in the room might bring to the process, what surprising discoveries we all might make together. A lot of my ideas don't pan out at all, but, surprisingly, quite a few do manage to survive. I keep checking back in with my main ideas at different points in rehearsal to make sure they aren't getting buried or lost, to make sure the play still has a shape, though often a somewhat different shape than I'd envisioned when everything was just flat on paper and in my head.

QUICK JUMP TO THE PHYSICAL   The urgency of all this brings us quickly to our feet. We don't really do "table work" at Ten Thousand Things; we don't spend days sitting and talking about the play. We take a little time when first starting to work on a scene to ask a lot of questions. The imagined audiences inform our questioning, encouraging us to ask obvious questions and intensifying our imagining of the depths, complexities, and urgency of the characters' situations. Actors in the cast with past Ten Thousand Things experience are easily able to summon up an audience of female inmates or the crowd at Dorothy Day to help imagine a moment; they can easily go deeper when they realize they will be held accountable by a male inmate who has lived the very experience they are trying to create onstage. Our audiences are a vast resource in the rehearsal room as we begin to ask questions. We feel no pressure to answer any of them right away. I put my ignorance front and center, sprinkling many "I don't knows" into the question session, encouraging the actors to do the same.

After about an hour or so of asking and floating questions about a scene, we get on our feet. We've found we can only really begin to understand our work when it begins to enter our bodies. Experiencing the reality of each situation through the body, we've found, just gets at the truth much more quickly than sitting around, talking and talking. The work of a Ten Thousand Things actor is very physical, and I want to start tapping into the energy and knowledge of each actor's body as soon as possible. As the actors begin to feel the scene out on their feet, I find myself getting up and moving around, too, trying to feel things in my body as well. Moving, I like to watch what happens to actors' bodies and how they position themselves in relation to one another. I rely very much on their physical instincts and impulses, often just adjusting here and there to help make the storytelling clearer.

HIGH STAKES   We worked to make the urgency of the first scene of *Midsummer,* when the lovers must make their cases before the Duke, very high. Our imagined audiences, living at life's extremes, helped. When the Duke pronounced that Hermia's penalty for disobeying her mother's wishes would be death, the actors were able to jump very quickly to the severity of this reality. Having Lysander and Hermia be a same-sex couple also helped to raise the stakes, so the whole situation of facing severe punishment simply for falling in love with the wrong person became more believable. We decided that homosexuality would not be an issue in this world, that Egeus's objections to Lysander marrying her daughter had nothing to do with the fact that they were both women—she just preferred Demetrius. But the echoes and resonance with our own world, where same-sex couples still face dangers, were inescapable; the whole situation became more real and more heartbreaking. Gay marriage had just won a triumphant victory in the state of Minnesota, so the issue was very timely.

In that first scene, we also tried to take Helena, a character who is often trivialized and ridiculed, seriously. Helena has been betrayed by Demetrius, who has suddenly asked Hermia, her best friend, to marry him. We chose to highlight how Helena's deep friendship with Hermia helps her to overcome any jealous feelings she might have toward her friend. We thought it more interesting to watch her struggle with her feelings and finally push them aside, rather than easily and thoughtlessly venting her jealousy. This portrait of the possibilities for depth in women's friendship also proved refreshing.

Once we start to grasp the emotional depths of the situations in a scene, our audiences next demand we turn our attention to the storytelling. The experienced actors in the room know the painful consequences of a story not being clear. Brightly lit faces full of boredom, restlessness, and confusion do not make good acting partners.

CREATING FOCUS   The most important part of clear storytelling is actually about creating focus. I pay a great deal of attention to exactly what I want the audience to focus on every moment. We have very few resources with which to create focus: actors' bodies, the occasional prop, as well as strong actions that can be felt underneath the words. Sounds, of course, also help to create focus, and Peter and I, once a scene starts taking shape, begin to layer in the sounds that will cause audiences to focus their attention: on exits and entrances, of course, but also on words we really want them to hear, gestures we really want them to see, lines we really want to resonate. For *Midsummer*, with all its magic, Peter had a real workout. Sound is really the only way we have to suggest magic is happening on our little bare stage: a stroke on a gong, a crotales, or a cymbal, a run on the high wind chimes. I love to watch an audience to see how little it takes to make them believe that a spell has been cast, a dream has been entered, magic has occurred. Most of the time the entranced audience is completely unaware of Peter's acrobatic efforts just off to the side.

Even actors' eyes can be used as spotlights to create focus. I'm serious. Sometimes during a particularly challenging line, I find I have nothing else at my disposal to help the audience understand what is going on than the eyes of the actor who is listening to the line. Having his eyes shift on a certain word can cause our very close audience to focus on what I want them to hear. Creating focus is all about causing people to pay attention—and paying attention is the essence of feeling alive.

One of the most important discoveries we've made about storytelling is that just because a character *says* something doesn't mean anyone in the audience has heard it. A playwright may weave a telling detail into a character's speech, and the character may say it, but that still doesn't mean it's been heard. Sound, emphasis, speed, and gestures are the tools we have to make sure that audiences hear the important things we want them to hear.

Another important part of storytelling is momentum and pacing. Nothing extraordinary about this either, though I think the extreme life situations of our audiences make us even more aware of the importance of moving things along. Experienced Ten Thousand Things actors know that, in the high-stakes world we inhabit, there is little room for emotional indulgence. We have felt too many audiences become restless and bored when an actor takes the time to pause and cry for even ten seconds. No one really wants to watch someone cry for very long. There are too many more important things to be done.

And I must say, using all these elements, I feel we were able to make the storytelling in *Midsummer* crystal clear, particularly in the often very confusing first scene. We replaced pronouns with names, actors gestured toward the person being spoken about. Actors found the right times to move toward or away from each other, punctuated with sharp sound, all bringing focus to who and what was being discussed. The high stakes added to the focus, of course, and demanded that everything move right along, giving no one time to indulge. I honestly felt we were able to make that first scene one of the clearest openings of a Shakespeare play we'd ever done. In performance, the rapt attention of almost every audience during this scene, bodies leaning forward, faces deeply concerned, really confirmed that the focus was working.

STORYTELLING BETWEEN SCENES As the four and a half weeks of rehearsal passed, I kept checking back to the original common human experiences I hoped we would illuminate through the play. And ironically, given the title of this chapter, I must confess that during rehearsals I got a little too caught up in one of my ideas, even though it had come from necessity. My desire to highlight the experience of how we "sleepwalk through enormous changes in our lives" grew a little cumbersome. I had originally imagined that for every scene change we would watch all the pajamaed actors drop the costume pieces from one world and put on new ones in a sleeplike trance, standing around outside the circle as they changed. We spent quite a bit of time trying to make this happen, hammering away with sounds to punctuate, but it just wasn't working. It all felt tedious and slow. I finally realized, by way of an actor's helpful comment, that it was pretty much impossible to create focus around the entire outside of the circle since the audience can only see part of it at any one time. People just naturally look to the center of the circle instead. So I dropped that idea. Instead, in between scenes, we told one little sleepwalking story inside the playing area while the other actors changed their costumes quickly outside the circle, unnoticed. With no blackouts, scene changes become one of the most important resources we have to make the storytelling clear.

We didn't have to toss out all the work we'd done. The play still began with actors sleepwalking into the circular playing area—with dreamy chimes and sounds—in their eclectic dark blue and gray pajamas. Before the show, we placed the red and purple satin robes of the nobles and lovers on the floor of the circle. One actor stopped suddenly (with a drum thump) when he was about to step on a crown. The actor looked down, saw it, and slowly bent to pick it up, feeling the transformation that occurred when he put it on his head. He became Theseus. The other actors did the same with the robes they stopped in front of, bending to slip them on, transforming into the characters of the nobility. Couples reached out for one another and drifted offstage in pairs; the older actress who had become Egeus, Hermia's mother, followed Hermia and her female lover offstage with concern. The actress playing Hippolyta started to head offstage alone, but Theseus, still in slow motion, took hold of her arm and pulled her back across the stage through the palace gates, giving a clear sense that she was an unwilling partner. One last actress entered, late, in her pajamas, carrying the silver moon/hillock across the stage, then placing it down in between the aluminum pillars to become the steps into the palace. She turned to discover that only one costume was left on the floor: a servant's jacket and hat. Slowly and with great disappointment, she put it on, becoming Philostrate, heading up the steps into the palace with a sigh.

This storytelling about sleepwalking through big changes continued in the transitions. We focused on just one or two actors at a time instead of all of them. At the end of the first scene, we saw the actor who had been stuck with the role of Philostrate the servant step back out on the palace steps to look at the moon, filled with a yearning to play a bigger part. She spotted a roughly woven brown vest and hat in one of the aisles and crossed to change costumes to become Bottom. As Bottom, she could play *all* the good parts! In the next transition, as all the Rude Mechanicals scurried away, Hippolyta stepped out of the palace to gaze at the moon. She too was filled with a yearning to play a part other than that of a captive bride. Puck scurried across the stage and dropped Oberon's black robes in the center, and the actress, surrounded by dream chimes, changed costumes and roles with pleasure and relief. The empty yard outside the palace transformed into the strange and beleaguered forest as goblins scampered in with the trees and hillocks, all to eerie night sounds.

Thus we proceeded through the scene changes of the play, sometimes telling the story of an actor sleepwalking into a new reality and sometimes just telling the actual story of the play more clearly. For example, we used a doll puppet as the changeling child, to help to make that difficult story clearer. In a later transition, we were able to watch Oberon steal the changeling from Titania, unnoticed, as she and Bottom passed by completely enamored with one another.

I think all our work on the transitions paid off, not only in clarifying the story but in allowing the audience to consider "sleepwalking through life." One of my favorite comments came after a performance at a detox center, when a woman came up to us and said, "I liked how the actors played lots of parts. I've played lots of parts in my life, too, most of them really shitty ones." Sometimes we heard audience members making comments like, "Uh-oh, that

Sun Mee Chomet as Oberon with tree trunk, *A Midsummer Night's Dream*, Avalon School, 2013.

one's going to fall asleep again!" It seemed to attune everyone more clearly to the times when characters in the actual story, like Bottom waking up from her dream, for example, or Titania from hers, were making transitions between realities of their own.

There was one transition I do wish I could have figured out how to make clearer. In Act IV, when our King Oberon stepped out of the goblin world and went back to being the captive bride Hippolyta while Queen Titania returned to being Theseus, I wanted to make it clear how each had been affected by their experiences in the goblin world as a member of the opposite sex. Each had suddenly experienced having a lot more or a lot less power. Our double-casting required a lightning-fast change because one second after Oberon and Titania leave the slumbering lovers in the forest, Theseus and Hippolyta are supposed to enter the same spot. We would have to watch the costume change, so I decided to have it happen as they sleepwalked around the outside of the circle, dropping their goblin clothes and picking up their royal ones as they exited the forest on one side and reentered from the other. It never worked. The audience never paid attention to the actors walking outside the circle, and the impact of this important transition was almost always lost. I can now see it would have been so much better just to have them change their costumes in the center of the stage, right in the middle of the forest full of sleeping lovers. We could have watched their wonder at their transformation so clearly then. But this became just another of the many mistakes I've made over all these years, discovering what would work better from watching audiences and shows over and over again.

AD LIBS   When I cast a Ten Thousand Things show, in addition to finding the very best and most diverse actors, I place enormous weight on assembling a group of people who are also kind, generous, and playful. The tour can be unpredictable and challenging, and the actors need to be able to approach each performance with complete trust of one another. Even one selfish or unaware actor can make the tour almost unbearably hard. With *Midsummer*, I had certainly assembled such a kind and generous cast—and one that was even more playful than usual.

One of the most unexpected discoveries of rehearsals was the surprising ad libs and asides the actors came up with. This hadn't ever really happened in our Shakespeare work before, but something about the strangeness of this play and its story, along with the camaraderie of the cast, seemed to inspire it. Several of the actors had worked with Ten Thousand Things many times before, and being very familiar with our audiences, in rehearsal they just naturally started making little comments to the empty seats. Karen Wiese-Thompson, a large, middle-aged woman playing Puck, modeled the goblin on the behavior of her son as a teenager and began to mutter lots of comments under her breath, questioning Oberon's commands with, "Seriously?" "Are you kidding me?" Sun Mee Chomet, new to Ten Thousand Things and playing both Hippolyta and Oberon, was eager to connect with our audiences and, inspired by Karen, began to comment occasionally to the audience as well. I recall one moment in particular when Sun Mee, who had been struggling a bit with the goblin King role, decided in the middle of one of Oberon's tirades to pick up one of the aluminum tree trunks and start to thrust with it as a phallus. This action seemed to release a huge energy, both in herself and in the rest of the cast, a sexual energy to be sure, but also an enormously playful one that never left rehearsals or performances thereafter.

Elise Langer, a younger, petite woman playing Bottom, brought all her clowning skills front and center, inspiring all the other Rude Mechanicals to make lively little comments as they worked on their play about Pyramus and Thisbe. Kurt Kwan, who played Demetrius, Mustardseed, and Flute, the lone male of our Rude Mechanicals who finds himself cast as the heroine Thisbe, was an astonishing source of inventiveness throughout rehearsals, delighting us every day with something new. Early on, he came up to me privately and said, "Flute doesn't want to play a woman, but once he decides to accept the part, he decides he's going to be the best damn woman he can be." Kurt had Flute draw on whatever sparse ideas of women he had, largely from pop culture. Flute began to incorporate the movements of Beyoncé into his dialogue, as well as twerking at various key moments.

I was a little concerned about the number of ad libs and asides and sometimes reined them in a bit, not wanting them to overwhelm the play. But a playful spirit had clearly been set loose, and after our first few performances, where our audiences of female inmates were almost riotous with laughter, I really could see how the ad libs, rather than detracting, opened up the world of the play still wider and allowed the audience to feel connected to the characters and enter in more completely. The ad libs wouldn't have worked if the audience hadn't been following the story clearly. A few of the critics who attended our paying shows seemed to be a bit taken aback by the unorthodoxy of it (we often have great fun watching the critics' faces in our fully lit performances, something they are not used to). We could see a few of them resist joining in the merriment, and one or two voiced their disapproval in reviews. I don't think I would have let the actors ad lib so much with most other Shakespeare plays. But *Midsummer* was a strange beast, and over and over again our experience was that the little off-hand remarks only served to welcome and pull the audience, traditional and nontraditional alike, even more deeply into this very strange world. When an inmate came up to us afterward and proclaimed, "That was dope as hell!" I couldn't help but think that Shakespeare, whose plays were full of asides, and his actors, quite used to the open comments of the groundlings, would have approved.

NO TECH   Though this chapter was meant to focus on preparation and rehearsals, it's hard to write about a production without including at least some of the responses of our audiences. Seeing *Midsummer* afresh through the eyes of our delighted first-time audiences helped us all to discover what a very weird and strange story Shakespeare decided to tell. But I'd like to end the chapter in much the same place we end all our rehearsals. After three and a half weeks of working on scenes and piecing them together, we spend another week running the show five times, once a day. Although I usually refer to this as our "birthing week," where concentration has to be particularly focused and intense, what is especially delightful about these final run-throughs is that we have no need for technical rehearsals. There is no interruption to the flow of the acting discoveries by taking long days to work on lighting cues. Our lighting—the sound—is already in place (though sometimes we take part of a rehearsal to go through all the sound cues). Because we have no tech, we are able to maintain our focus on deepening the acting and clarifying the storytelling.

After our final run-through, we load up the van. We all look at each other. We are teetering on a brink, with our play halfway completed. People in any production feel this way before opening night, of course. But at Ten Thousand Things, this sense of teetering on the brink of the unknown is perhaps even more intense. Our nontraditional audiences generally know more about the world of the play than we do. It's why humility is a keystone of the rehearsal process. We stand on the precipice of possibly the most humbling moment of all. We've tried the best we can to imagine the audience. Now we set off to meet them face to face and see how well we've done.

Sarah Agnew in *Carousel*, Skyline Housing, 2004.

NO PLACE TO HIDE
Performances

ON THE FIRST DAY OF REHEARSAL, we begin our focus on the audience with veteran performers sharing tales of favorite exhilarating and excruciating performance moments. We have an endless supply:

TALES OF PAIN . . .   There are always plenty of excruciating stories. In fact, many actors describe these quite painful experiences with a kind of glee, celebrating them as survivors celebrate battle scars, relishing the looks of consternation that often appear on the faces of the novices. And every such story still brings up a tiny clench in my muscles, making me want to hunch over and avert my eyes, just as I most likely did at the time of the incident. The time, for example, with *Measure for Measure* in a women's prison, when we found ourselves with eight minutes left of the show but only four minutes away from "count": the exact moment when, no matter what, the bell would ring, the show would have to stop, and the audience would immediately be herded back to their cells by the guards. Miraculously, the actors managed to barrel through to the end with seconds to spare. Or showing up to perform *Richard III* in a men's shelter, we discovered that the empty and peaceful large room we had previewed during the day became a hotbed of personal territorial battles at night, with each man fiercely marking out his regular squares of linoleum for his sleeping bag and few belongings. Many of the men were very unhappy, of course, that we were occupying their spaces with our stage area and our props. We learned there were no chairs for the audience to sit on and there was no other separate room for men who didn't want to watch the show to retreat to. Many had food to heat in the corner microwave. Shouts of "Hey, that's *my* mac and cheese!" punctuated the show. Or the time when we took *Red Noses* to a juvenile correctional facility and, facing a restless, overcrowded room of kids just moments before the time the show absolutely had to begin so it could end in time to avoid a mass exodus at the very loud lunch bell, we learned that the van with our set, props, and musical instruments was stuck in gridlock traffic on a highway several miles away. We had no choice but to plunge in anyway, improvising props from car keys and pencils (slowly sneaking set pieces onto the stage once the van finally arrived). Or most recently on our *Music Man* tour, the cast was heartbroken when the production, which had wildly delighted audiences of both male and female inmates, met with a cold, almost hostile reception at the final women's prison on the tour. The performance was so painful to plow through, having to constantly look at the rows of unfriendly faces. Near the end, we were able to figure out that the presence of a male videographer we had hired to record the show had made the women very suspicious, defensive, and even angry. That won't happen again. The excruciating performances we've had on our tours seem truly endless, and the stories could easily fill a volume of their own. But despite the pain, these experiences have also been blessings, each one teaching us something important about what works and what to avoid.

EXTERNAL CONDITIONS   Many, if not most, of our excruciating performances are caused by actual performance conditions at the sites, which are often beyond our control. In the early days of the company, when I was doing everything myself—grant writing, budgeting, tour planning, as well as directing and raising a toddler—I would hear of a promising place for a performance and make arrangements by phone, trusting that everything would work out. Then we showed up at a women's shelter to discover we were expected to perform *The Emperor of the Moon* in the kitchen, a space no more than eight feet wide lined with enormous refrigerators and stoves. That was one of the few shows we actually had to cancel.

SCOUTING THE SITE   Over the years, we have learned ways to try to minimize the chance of a disaster. First, we scout each site. We have to scope it out to make sure there's a room that is large enough for our fifteen-by-fifteen-foot square or circular playing area, the rings of chairs, and an aisle behind the last row for the actors to travel around. Large conference rooms work wonderfully well; gyms are challenging acoustically, though they are often the only available option. In cafeterias, we have to be sure pillars won't get in the way too much. But if we want to reach a particular audience badly enough, we can be creative in how we adapt.

BUILT-IN AUDIENCES   Next, we have to make sure there will actually be an audience. This means we have to be sure that the audience will already be there. We very quickly learned that putting up flyers announcing a performance, with the expectation that people will make a special trip to the site at a special time, never works. Never. People who haven't seen theater before are very reluctant to go out of their way to do so. Even crossing a parking lot from the residential building of a homeless shelter to the cafeteria in a separate building is too big a distance to travel. We have to "capture" our audience when they are already at the space, at a time when there isn't too much else to do.

VISIBLE EMPTY SEATS   And we want to have an audience because, quite simply, with all the lights on, we can see all the empty seats, and it hurts. Audience members are our acting partners, and unfilled chairs mean our acting partners haven't shown up. We can't mute their absence as actors performing to a darkened house can. It quickly becomes very clear how profoundly actors need the pushback of an audience's energies; the glaringly obvious empty seats feel like black holes. The absence of the audience is a primal experience.

Luckily, the fluid "architectural design" of our theater space allows us to alleviate some of the pain of empty seats. We can simply remove all the empty chairs. As long as the front row is filled (usually about twenty-four to twenty-eight people fit around the playing space, six or seven to a side), we can remove chairs in the second or third rows. The front row is crucial. If most people decide to sit in the second or third row but the front is largely empty, the energy drain is very noticeable. We have become masters at harnessing the audience's energy through seating arrangements, with lots of encouragement

Women's correctional facility, *Ragtime*, 2005.

as they enter the space: "Front row seats are the best! Try them: you can see everything from there!" If we sense that despite our best efforts a particular audience will want to "hide" in the second or third row—or that more than a few dozen people may not show up, we only put out a front row, forcing everyone to sit up front, adding seats only as additional bodies enter the room. No matter what, though, we do need enough bodies to fill up that first row, and there have been times when even two dozen people don't show.

We once set up in the lobby of a low-income senior center for a 7 PM show, only to learn that no one was coming because everyone had already gone to bed. We planned for an afternoon show at a men's shelter and not one homeless person showed up. We learned that, although early Sunday afternoon had been identified as the time most likely to draw the biggest audience, the staff had forgotten that the NCAA playoffs were on TV; there was just no way any of the men were crossing the street to the church gym to see *Cymbeline*. Once at a homeless shelter, we were about three-quarters of the way through the play and a horde of people started to stream into the room for their dinner, making it almost impossible for the actors to shout above the din to finish the play. We quickly learned we needed to schedule shows there so that they were done by 4 PM. Clearly, knowledge of the intricacies of just how each site actually works, including the exact time of day and the exact day of the week when a potential audience will actually be present, is essential to properly filling the chairs.

STAFF AS ALLIES This is where the next crucial component of a successful performance comes into play—one enthusiastic staff member. When we're scouting, checking for that large-enough room, we always have our radar out for that one person on staff who "gets it," who truly understands how rewarding the experience could be for those with whom they work. Someone who is willing to put in some "coaxing time," encouraging people on an individual basis: "Come on, you should try it. I promise you it won't be boring. These guys are great, such good actors. You have to give it a chance!" Talking it up every day, often for a period of several weeks before the show, takes a lot of persistence, patience, and energy from staff who are already often stressed from the demands of their thinly funded low-income centers.

Luverne Seifert, *Man of La Mancha*, women's correctional facility, 2011.

It is vital to always remember how strong the resistance to seeing theater is among most people who've never experienced it. This took me a good while to truly understand. In the early days, before I'd really realized what a vital ally the right staff person could be, I tried to drum up enthusiasm among resistant potential audience members myself, coaxing and pleading, marching up and down empty hallways to knock on doors before the show began. Once at a soup kitchen we were confident that we had found the right time of day to perform, just after noon, when the cafeteria was still full. But when it was announced with a microphone that "There will be a play after lunch," people looked up in consternation, gobbled down their meals, and fled. (It turned out that, because it was a Catholic soup kitchen, people were afraid it would be a bad reenactment of some kind of religious tract.) During our very first women's prison show, a weary voice announced over the public address system, "You can come see a play in the cafeteria now, or you can stay in your cell." The "enthusiasm" of this announcement managed to motivate about fifteen women to straggle down the halls. (Those fifteen women by the way, turned out to be one of our all-time favorite audiences, with their unrestrained responses to Fornés's *Mud*.)

We relearn the value of that staff advocate whenever one is absent. When the beloved volunteer coordinator at a county prison system was sick, we showed up to do *Carousel* at the men's facility, which at the time allowed no chairs in the gym, only mats on the floor. Only ten men showed up for the performance. We later learned that an unsympathetic guard had arbitrarily decided his entire cell block would be unable to attend. Our volunteer coordinator would ordinarily have known how to handle this situation and work around the guard. We carried on, more people in the cast than in the audience, the men lying on the mats like it was preschool nap time, though usually awake and thoroughly enjoying themselves. We enjoyed ourselves, too, once we got over the initial surprise and relaxed. Somehow the bodies stretched out on the mats filled the empty space—and it was weirdly fun to have to perform for such a low eye level. Another time a beloved contact at a state maximum-security facility died suddenly, and we learned that we would no longer be allowed into the prison. Only then did we fully realize how crucial this one man had been in navigating the difficult prison bureaucracy. It took us several years to find another person on staff who "got it" and would be able to work the system to allow us back in.

People often ask us how we "get into prison." In Minnesota it hasn't been that hard, especially at the county level. When I first approach program officers or volunteer coordinators with the idea of bringing in a play, many are puzzled but willing to give it a try, especially because it is free. Usually, once they see the enthusiasm of inmates for the work, they become allies. Now we even have guards at some prisons who schedule their shifts so they will be able to stand and watch the show while they're "on duty."

MIXED AUDIENCES   We've also found another way to hedge against the possibility of empty seats. In case a nontraditional audience just doesn't show up despite our and the staff members' best efforts, we invite members of the regular theatergoing public to come to these community sites as well. Many of our paying audience members are very curious to see what happens at a nontraditional site and willingly travel to unfamiliar locations. These shows are free, so it's easy to guarantee that at least several dozen seats at every location will be filled. It's discouraging, of course, when very few from the target low-income community show up and we find ourselves just performing for people who could have afforded to buy a ticket, but at least we've made sure that front row won't be empty. Indeed, at one point the danger became that regular theatergoers might overwhelm our community sites. We were doing *Ragtime* at a battered women's shelter, and over ninety regular patrons showed up. When the dozen or so residents of the shelter came down on the elevator to the performance room, they were startled to see so many strange faces and they quickly pushed the buttons to close the elevator doors and go back up to their rooms. Another kind of excruciating performance situation was born, when the people we wanted to perform for didn't feel welcome or comfortable in their own space. So we began to limit the number of free seats we made available to the general public, taking reservations beforehand. Those seats are now all snapped up right away.

With any venue, it takes time to figure out the details. Often, our first performance at a site doesn't work because, despite our best efforts, we don't hit on the right time or the staff member wasn't able to work up the enthusiasm she'd hoped. Very few spaces are perfect, so it's always a balancing act, taking into account our desire to reach a potentially very interesting audience and balancing it with the amount of uncontrollable chaos that seems to be inherent in the space.

UNTAMABLE CHAOS   Sometimes the chaos is just too much. Indeed, once we start performing, I often find myself shifting from being concerned about the audience to being concerned about the performers. I feel fiercely protective of them, wanting to do whatever I can to make the conditions as friendly toward their efforts as possible. And we certainly have encountered situations that we all agree are just too challenging, times when we decide we need to sever the relationship and give up. The actors often surprise me by how much they

Jim Lichtscheidl,
At Your Service,
Hubbs Center for
Lifelong Learning,
2005.

are willing to endure. We once did a performance of *Stones in His Pocket* at a homeless shelter in the winter. Because of the cold weather, the actors in this small two-man show found themselves acting in a huge room in the midst of hundreds of people who were there only because of the temperature outside, not because they wanted to see the play. I could barely watch. Whenever I did manage to raise my head and peek out, I could at least spot a few people sitting in the inner rings who seemed quite delighted and caught up in the story. I approached the actors after the show full of apologies, but one of them, the always astonishing Steve Epp, interrupted me, almost panting with pride, exclaiming, "It was like performing in the Theater Olympics! The amount of concentration and focus we had to give each other, I loved it!" Nevertheless, we will not perform at that shelter in the winter again, and we will only perform shows with large casts, who can counterbalance the energies of the always somewhat chaotic room.

We also learned that doing two shows in one day is too much. We were performing *In a Garden*, two mini-operettas by Gertrude Stein and one by local playwright Kevin Kling. The pieces blended together to create a gleeful celebration of childlike playfulness and mischief, something I had noticed all of our audiences hunger for at some level. I had cast three extremely jubilant, inventive actors who somehow made it all work. But one afternoon the actors performed for an audience of over a hundred men at a maximum-security prison. Then, just a few hours later, they found themselves performing at a women's shelter for an audience of toddlers, dropped off after dinner by their mothers who had thought it was a children's play. Maximum-security prisoners and toddlers in one day. The inmates, of course, took quite a bit of coaxing to get to any kind of playful, silly place, while the toddlers became frightened at some of the adult matters in the operetta, upsetting their mothers as well. It was all much too much. The three actors now proudly tell this battle tale with great hilarity, but this will never be a company that asks its actors to do eight shows a week.

NOT EVERY SHOW FOR EVERY AUDIENCE   There are also excruciating shows caused not just by challenging performance conditions but by a mismatch

ALL THE LIGHTS ON

of material and audience. We know, of course, despite our best efforts to find "big enough fairy tales," that certain stories just aren't going to interest teen audiences and others probably won't interest senior citizens. We've decided that Shakespeare is just too much for English language learners (though we've had people come up to us after such performances and tell us that although they couldn't understand much, they could hear the beauty of the poetry). We now have a roster of over fifty different possible venues in the Twin Cities, five or six of which we return to with almost every show, like the county prisons or a few large homeless shelters, because their populations are so transient, it's largely a new crowd each time. From the rest of the roster, we try to choose other groups that might respond especially strongly to each particular play, and we now add two or three shows in a rural community to each tour as well.

But sometimes there is still a big misfire. In our earliest years, we performed María Irene Fornés's *Mud* at an adult education center. In more than one scene, the character Lloyd talks about how he likes to fuck pigs. The adult audience clearly relished the language, along with the respect it conveyed to them as being adults who could, of course, handle such material. But the teachers were livid. Many came up afterward to tell us how upset the language had made them; one teacher hissed, "What's the name of your company again? Ten Thousand Swear Words?" Since then I've had ample time to consider that we are intruders—we are always performing in someone else's space, and it is important to be respectful of this. Though we will never censor any material, we now are mindful of how some institutions, especially those that work with youth, are trying to encourage respectful language in their spaces. So, before agreeing to a performance, we warn staff that the play contains challenging language and allow them to make their own decision about whether they want us to come.

VOLUNTARY AUDIENCES   It is also critical to note that we only perform for voluntary audiences. Even in prisons, we are clear that we do not want to perform for people who have been compelled to attend. Usually there is an advance sign-up sheet for inmates who are interested, and sometimes attending a play becomes a kind of privilege. Once or twice, staff have either forgotten or ignored these requirements, and the result is disastrously painful for everyone. The audience is suspicious and hostile, but the actors have no choice but to perform for them. For this reason, we don't do "school shows," where students are required by their teachers to come, although sometimes we will perform at a school during after hours. We usually only perform for one or two youth groups per tour, however. The work of Ten Thousand Things is primarily for adults, as the plays we regularly choose to do are based on intensely adult experiences of life. And we've learned that already self-conscious teens often don't respond well to the fully lit intimacy of our performances.

THE INTRODUCTION A little advance warning right before the play begins can go a long way in easing the bumps along the road. One of the most crucial components of any performance, be it for a nontraditional or a paying audience, has become "The Introduction." It's usually just a few sentences. In my love of getting to the essence, I put a great deal of care into finding the fewest words needed to give any audience member the right context to have it all make sense. Most of our nontraditional audiences show up at a performance without having any idea of what the play is about, unlike paying audiences who have usually had a chance to read about a show in the paper and choose among shows to find the one that most appeals. Program notes don't work. Many in our audiences don't know how to read, and those who can often don't know that information about time and setting can be found in the program. Besides such basics, I try to provide one hook or one question that might interest people in what is to come. I usually don't know what these sentences are until a day or two before we open, and it usually takes one or two performances to refine it perfectly. For *The Seven*, Will Power's retelling of Aeschylus's *The Seven Against Thebes*, for example, I simply said, "This is the story of two brothers who take over a kingdom, vowing to share it and rule it peacefully together, and all the things that get in the way of their doing this." I added that it was a story that was more than two thousand years old, originally from ancient Greece, and was now being retold by a living writer in hip-hop style. Just those two sentences were enough to orient the audience and spark their interest. For *Measure for Measure*, I ended up just giving the brilliant summary presented to me by a homeless man at intermission during a shelter show: "This is really a lot like that TV show *Undercover Boss!*" I added that in the play, a duke decides to put one of her deputies in charge and go into hiding, disguising herself so she can spy on her employees to see what happens in her absence. Those few sentences were all it took.

The Introduction can also be very effective at calming and centering an audience, allaying their suspicions and fears. With Shakespeare, for example, I always note that it takes any audience, no matter how many times they've seen Shakespeare before, five minutes or so to get used to how the characters talk, but I promise that if people hang on, everything will soon become very clear. The relief is palpable; our veteran audiences breathe more easily as well.

The Introduction can also help to shape an audience's energies—again, with just a sentence or two—even displacing the misogyny we so often wrestle with in men's prisons, especially in plays with sexual content. One of our most excruciating moments came during a performance of *Othello* at a men's county jail, where the men started cheering as Othello strangled Desdemona. Chances are that's what the groundlings did, too, during Shakespeare's time, but it was profoundly upsetting to all of us, especially the actress playing Desdemona. Usually, the misogyny isn't quite as overt, but when it's there, it always puts us on edge.

Over time, we've come to see such misogyny as honesty about feelings that many men have but which some have just learned to hide better than others. Although we much prefer the men's prison shows where it isn't present, its open expression gives us a chance for a conversation about it through our performance. Just recently, with our production of *A Streetcar Named Desire*, I think I finally hit upon the right words in the Introduction to rein it in. *Streetcar* is replete with moments of a man being cruel and abusive to his wife and his sister-in-law. I started out noting that we did three plays a year at the facility and thanked the men for always being a good audience. (I've learned not to ask how many have seen a show before, as many are reluctant to admit how long they've been in prison.) Then I mentioned that I was sure they knew how much concentration and focus acting takes, especially with the audience so close up, and added that there were several scenes in this play that were particularly challenging for the two actresses. Not only did this perk the men's interest, but I could feel their energy shift from being dismissive of the female characters to being protective of them. They were attentive and respectful throughout the entire play. We were able to have a great discussion with them afterward, too, about Stanley's slapping of Stella, getting their thoughts on why she would want to go back to him, as well as their judgments of whether Blanche should have been sent to a mental institution (many of them saw her as quite strong and resilient). We'll see if this Introduction solution holds up as time goes on.

The Introduction is also a supremely useful tool for preparing experienced, paying audiences for what they are about to see. As discussed, these audiences bring their own expectations, which can serve as barriers. One thing we finally figured out, after several years of finding paying audiences to be so much stiffer than nontraditional ones, is that they expect to sit in the dark. It makes them really uncomfortable to be so exposed, seated in a circle with all the lights on. Ever since, I always mention that we're going to leave the lights on and point out that not only will the actors be able to see them (noting how much the actors enjoy this, compared to playing to a dark house) but that everyone else will be able to see them and that this awareness may make them uncomfortable for a bit but that they will quickly forget about it and come to enjoy watching everyone else as part of the show.

More important, I use these introductions as a way to help paying audiences to understand our work, listing all the different places we have performed and describing some of the responses of our nontraditional audiences. This not only calms and centers the paying audience, but you can see, during the performance, that they start to imagine the play through the eyes of others, others who are from quite different circumstances. You can almost hear them start to ask, "What would a homeless woman think of that scene? How would an inmate have reacted to that line?" Seeing the world through the eyes of others is the principle act of theater. And this act can be multiplied geometrically with our paying audiences, all because of a few simple sentences in the Introduction.

ALL THE LIGHTS ON

DESPITE OUR BEST EFFORTS Excruciating performances still happen. On every tour. Less frequently than in the early years, of course, but frequently enough so that we have all learned to embrace them as a necessary part of the work. It helps us to realize that, often, what has felt excruciating to us hasn't felt that way to many in the audience. Many people get sucked into the world of the play, no matter what the surroundings. And I always remind actors that ordinary dark houses shield them from so much. Were you to shine a spotlight on any audience at any big regional theater at any moment, you would always see restless bodies, hanging heads, yawning, tapping toes, bored looks.

With all the lights on, we must remember that outside appearances are so often deceptive. Take the audience of inmates who seemed so restless during *Antigone* but who leapt up into a three-minute standing ovation after the final line. Or our very first time at a mental health facility where we were to perform *The Most Happy Fella*. We were full of nerves beforehand, imagining that people might be erratic and irrational, jumping up to shout at unpredictable moments. In fact, it was like performing in the midst of a circle of absolutely motionless statues seated in wheelchairs; the audience was so highly medicated that their facial muscles didn't twitch. Our acting partners felt absent, and we experienced it as a very hard show. And yet afterward, as we were packing up, staff members rushed up to us with beaming faces, exclaiming that they had never seen their clients so engaged. They were clearly able to detect muscle movements that we were not—but their assurances were so surprised and heartfelt that we had to believe them. We probably won't do Shakespeare for such audiences, but now that we know what to prepare ourselves for, upcoming performances won't be so hard.

In every excruciating show, even those where most of the audience really is disengaged for whatever reason, even in those performances, no matter what, there are always at least a few people whom we touch profoundly. Actors can always look around the circle and find at least a few open and friendly faces to connect with for support. There are always a few who rush up to us after the show, exclaiming their surprise over how much they loved it, wondering how they might be able to take their families next time, almost always at least one comment like, "This is the best TV I ever saw," that can make us feel that even the excruciating show was somehow worth it.

Still, no matter what we learn later about how much seemingly disengaged audiences have actually loved the performance, in the moment such performances are really hard on the actors and on me. So we have invented the Cocktail Coupon. During each tour, if a very difficult show makes it feel necessary, Ten Thousand Things will take the whole cast out for drinks. At least there we can laugh and commiserate, and soon the whole painful ordeal retreats into our collective pantheon of good stories to share.

THE ONES THAT MAKE IT ALL WORTHWHILE For every excruciating performance there is an exhilarating one, the shows where the connection with the audience is profound. We usually have two or three of these on every tour as well, and, again, after so many years of touring, the stories could fill their own volume. But it is safe to say we will always remember the performance of *Ragtime* at a women's facility where the inmates, so many of them separated from their children, so completely identified with the character Sarah, the African American maid who ends up bearing the child of the jazz musician Coalhouse Walker. The women spoke out words of comfort when Sarah, abandoned by Coalhouse and with no land of her own, is caught burying her baby in the yard of a wealthy white woman. They sobbed and cried out her name when Sarah is shot by the police while trying to defend Coalhouse from his own unjust arrest, and they literally screamed with joy when the two reunite in the play's reprise of the musical number "Wheels of a Dream." It was a group catharsis the likes of which none of us had ever witnessed before. We will always remember the moment when, in *King Lear*, the usually humming people at the edge of the large homeless shelter room fell dead silent as Lear, in rags on the open heath, began to rant and rave at the cruelty of the passing storm. We will always remember the performance of the seventeenth-century commedia piece by Carlo Goldoni, *Il Campiello*, in a men's prison where almost every hardened face burst open into glee and then wonder, where men lined up afterward to shake the actors' hands, exclaiming that it was "the best damn shit they'd ever seen."

These shows are a huge part of the reason why it's so easy, despite all the challenge and difficulty and often pain of this work, to come back and do it again. In fact, it's hard to go back to "real theater" once you've experienced the intensity of the deep, unexpected connections between the lives of the audience and the life of the play. It is as "real" as theater gets.

Randy Reyes, *Il Campiello*, men's correctional facility, 2011.

10

THE POWER OF UNEXPECTED CONNECTION—POLITICAL THEATER
Going into the World

I AM THE FIRST TO ADMIT that I bristle at the labels "political" or "social justice" or "educational" when applied to theater. Because of my extreme sensitivity to hints of condescension, I will openly defy anyone who asks that Ten Thousand Things demonstrate how we "change people's lives." I think it is extremely difficult to change anyone, and I'm not sure I've ever seen any theater performance change someone in any significant or measureable way. Part of my ferocity comes from knowing that larger theaters with primarily upper-middle-class audiences are generally not asked to quantify how they change lives. They are not asked to provide data on how many people, as the result of watching a play, stopped drinking too much or beating their wives or robbing workers of fair pay or deceiving the public about the amount of pollution their businesses pour into the air. I resist any attempts to make Ten Thousand Things show how our work changes the behavior of low-income people.

I think theater becomes flattened and dead when plays try to change, to educate, or to deliver overtly political messages. I have never seen such "message theater" be very successful; I don't recall ever witnessing it directly change anyone's mind about an issue. Such theater, in my experience anyway, usually delivers its messages to people who already agree. Probably the best political theater I've ever experienced is comic, like that of the San Francisco Mime Troupe, which delivers its messages to large like-minded crowds in Bay Area parks with large doses of humor and satire. I would be surprised to learn the skits have ever changed anyone's mind, but at least they energize the base,

giving everyone a good laugh. Whenever political message theater tries to be "serious," it makes me feel trapped and smaller; sometimes the hammering away at messages makes me feel so confined that I actually get a headache. I don't like to be preached to; I like to figure things out for myself. And I firmly believe, from years of having to work through the initial suspicions and resistance of marginalized people, that most of them feel the same way. They don't want to be told what to think; they know in their bones that life has no easy answers. Such experiences have led me to passionately believe that theater works best when it is a place we go to ask questions, to experience issues from multiple perspectives and be challenged to broaden our sense of the possibilities of the world.

SPREADING THE WEALTH OF THEATER With all that said, I do think that Ten Thousand Things is political. Just not in the ordinary sense of the word. We are not political through the content of our plays. Our work is political first and foremost because of the way it is distributed. For me, the most pressing political issue facing our country and, indeed, our world is its hugely unequal

ALL THE LIGHTS ON

Men's correctional facility, *Il Campiello,* **2011.**

distribution of wealth. Theater is a wealth. Very few people have access to it. It is primarily available only to those with higher incomes, in addition to the education about how to access it—how to find out where theaters are, what shows are playing, whether those plays are done well or would even be of interest. Add in access to transportation, to child care, and to free time, along with schooling in how to dress for the theater and how to behave as an audience member. It is accessible to very few.

Ten Thousand Things radically alters the system of distribution of theater's wealth. We bring the highest excellence theater can offer directly *to* people, in spaces where they are already comfortable, instead of expecting them to come to us. When you do this, everything changes. Our politics are really as simple—and profound—as that. If all the arts were to think deeply about their distribution systems and then work hard to actually change them, the political ramifications would be profound.

THEATER OF EMPATHY   I also believe that much of what theater has to offer is fundamentally political but, again, not because of any messages in its plays. The wealth of this live experience we are distributing comes with what theater asks us to *do*, not what it says. Theater is inherently political because it asks you to practice one simple, fundamental activity: putting yourself in another's place. All theater asks this of us at some level. Whenever we engage with a character, we are seeing things through her eyes, not just our own. Sometimes this empathy work is not too demanding, and we find ourselves primarily identifying with just one character, the one who is most like us. Sometimes, in the best plays, we are compelled to look through the eyes of more than one character, many of whom are different from ourselves. When we experience some sort of connection with a character, we experience a momentary sense that we share something in common. The visceral experience of sharing something in common with someone we thought was entirely different is surprising. And surprise can start a shift. The hoe hits the hardened soil of our thought patterns, breaking it up a bit. The more surprising this discovery of the connection, the stronger the force of the hoe, the looser the soil becomes. Loose soil is more receptive to seeds. Perhaps later down the road, a seed will drop into it; perhaps still later, something new will sprout.

Or perhaps not. I think it is important to be very honest about the actual possibilities of theater. I agree with the British director Declan Donnellan, who once said, "The only social service theater provides is to make people bigger." This is theater's limitation—and its profound wealth. "Making people bigger," making a little more room inside ourselves to incorporate the experience of another, is really the most theater can do to be political—but this is actually a lot.

THE THEATER OF UNEXPECTED CONNECTIONS   In Ten Thousand Things productions, the power of discovering unexpected connections with those who seem unlike us, the power of radiant energy, is multiplied and magnified. Not only do we have a chance to experience the multiple viewpoints of many characters in the play but, with all the lights on, we are able to consider the differing viewpoints of the other audience members seated around the circle. Some of our very favorite performances are those "mixed" ones at social service centers, where people from the general public can also attend. There, people from very different economic classes sit next to each other, and this "audience viewpoint effect" gets magnified even more strongly. A corporate manager who is a veteran theatergoer might find herself sitting across from a homeless man. Their different reactions to different moments of the play force each other to consider different perspectives. The homeless man may laugh at a particular moment, and the manager, after considering it for a bit, discovers the humor, too. She becomes a little bigger. Then she may laugh at something, causing the homeless man to see the situation in a new light; he finds himself laughing, too. They might laugh together at certain moments. This similarity might also cause surprise, making each one open up a bit more. That the connections are unexpected make them that much more powerful. There is so much power in surprise. Indeed, it is a rare experience in our world when people from vastly different economic backgrounds sit across from or next to each other as equals. I have always noticed a kind of sweetness to these performances for "mixed" audiences, a kind of relaxation and openness that perhaps the common meeting place of the story and the imaginary world of the play provide.

Even with our homogenous audiences, where mixing of economic perspectives is hard to come by, whether at paying shows or in the prisons, there is the perspective of the "imagined other audience." With the help of a little prodding from my introduction, our paying audiences find themselves trying to imagine the play not only from the viewpoints of the faces immediately around them but, through imagination, from the perspective of someone who is an inmate or living in poverty. In a prison, inmates often ask us if the same play they are experiencing has been seen by people who have paid for their own tickets. They are impressed to know that those audiences are also experiencing it in exactly the same way, with no stage and all the lights on. They imagine why those who can pay might have wanted to come watch this show. The hoe strikes again and again; the soil is further loosened. Through unexpected connection, we create at least the potential for change.

Actually, all of this "political activity" is very personal. Being moved to step outside oneself, to experience a small surprising moment of personal connection with another who is different—this is not how we are normally taught to think of politics. But our audiences have taught me that this very personal interaction is actually at the heart and core of any true political change. Many people who have led hardscrabble lives, trying each day to survive, do not bring political lenses to the table. They often haven't had time to learn to think in terms of labels or frameworks like "capitalism" or "socialism," "Republican" or "Democrat," "left" or "right." They just experience and respond to situations directly in the moment, as individuals, without thinking of political frames.

If there is an imbalance of power in a scene, they experience it personally, as the characters in the play do. In *Measure for Measure*, when Lord Angelo tells Isabella she must sleep with him or he will execute her brother, everyone in a prison feels the abuse of power. Women quickly put themselves in Isabella's place. For many, it's very easy to do because they have actually been in that place themselves. Some male inmates, however, resist making the leap into Isabella's perspective, preferring to enjoy the power of Lord Angelo. When Angelo continues to press, though, some men become a little uncomfortable because they too have experienced abuses of power from those above. Some men start to imagine their sisters in such a situation. Some of the men are surprised into finding they understand how things feel to Isabella.

Several scenes later when Claudio asks Isabella to put herself in his place and try to imagine what it feels like to be facing execution and sudden death, she refuses to do so. The perspective of some of the women may then start to shift a bit—they had been fully on Isabella's side when she felt trapped, but they now have been asked to consider how Claudio feels, and they understand his desperation. Isabella feels a little heartless to them now because she can't understand her brother's plight. The connection of one's heart gets shifted around a bit more. Firm judgments one moment become less certain, a little looser still a few moments later. We've been forced to stretch, to become a little bigger in our understanding than we were just moments ago.

Real political change begins not from absorbing messages but from experiencing directly how things feel to someone different from oneself. We begin with respect for those in our audience who rarely experience respect. This makes them feel listened to. When people feel listened to by those who usually don't listen, they are more likely to reach out and try to listen to others who are different. When a character speaks directly from the heart, it becomes more likely that the listener will see a connection. The power of Ten Thousand Things' theatrical work is that much greater because it is all so unexpected. Our nontraditional audiences, who so often feel excluded from the rest of the world, feel included for a moment or two. They feel respected because they are *not* being preached to. It surprises them, and they become more open. And our paying audiences, who usually feel quite included in the world, are surprised to find that others whom they had imagined to be quite different from themselves have actually greatly enjoyed the excellent theater which they enjoy as well—indeed, that these different audiences have perhaps even enjoyed it more keenly and intensely. Those of means are surprised to find they have something in common with those less fortunate. Everyone's size is increased just a bit.

As I discussed before, Ten Thousand Things' bare-bones production style can also give people practice at seeing unexpected connections. When there are few objects onstage, abstracted from their usual realistic settings, it becomes easier to spot their similarities, easier to see surprising connections between unrelated things. This practice can extend to seeing connections between people who are seemingly completely unalike. Our hallmark double- and triple-casting, when the same actor is seen as an imperious judge one moment and, with only a minor costume change of hat and vest, a goofy barkeep the next, can serve as a visceral reminder of the common humanity that both characters share. It can strengthen our intuitive understanding that in acting to help others, we are actually helping ourselves.

REALIGNING PRIORITIES   There is yet another way that the work of Ten Thousand Things is political. It has to do with the way, within our own organization, we have reimagined how to distribute wealth and power. As an organization, our priorities for how we spend our money are different from those of many other theaters. We don't need a building, so we don't have to spend money on that—just a dozen or so weeks in a church basement for rehearsals at fifty dollars a week, plus renting the large room in a literary center for sixteen weekends for our paying audiences. We obviously don't have to spend money on lighting equipment, and our sets still come in under eight hundred dollars. With the list of expenses narrowed, it becomes easier to name our priorities. We don't need many of the other trappings of theater, but we do need the very best artists, those at the peak of their craft. Our priorities thus become very clear—we will spend our money on human creative energy, on people, and particularly on artists. We openly state this as our priority, and the radiance of this decision comes across onstage as artists feel respected and valued.

All of this "political activity" once again starts from necessity. Springing from the simple desire to find audiences who will deeply connect to stories, we are compelled to bring the work to them, thus redistributing the wealth of theater. Because we have so many different kinds of people in our audiences, our plays must reflect a multiplicity of perspectives that audiences are compelled to consider. Because we have no stage, the audience must define it by sitting in a circle or square, and because we have all the lights on, the audience is compelled to consider each other's perspectives. Because we cause people of very different life experiences to sit next to each other, they are forced to consider things from even more radically different perspectives than they would if they were sitting in a more homogenous group. Because we can't carry a lot of stuff, the few objects onstage must serve different purposes and cause people to more easily see metaphors and connections between unlikely objects. And because we must strip down to essentials in doing our work, really only needing excellent artists, our spending priorities become very clear. The political work of Ten Thousand Things all centers on redistributing wealth, both the actual financial wealth of our organization and the wealth our art form affords. Through theater, we share more fairly the wealth of the opportunity to consider a situation through the eyes of others. We offer more fairly the opportunity to experience theater's radiant energy and its loosening up of hardened soils within, the ways it can make one become a little "bigger." All of this is political work. It all serves to increase, at least a little, the radiance of our world.

The author and her daughter.

ALL THE LIGHTS ON—FACING MISOGYNY AND REINVENTING DEAD SYSTEMS
Organic Organization

WHEN I WAS SURVEYING the very male world of directing in the 1990s, I could sense fairly quickly not only that I was a misfit but that it would be disastrous for me to even try to fit in. The few times I put my foot on one of the paths available to young directors, it almost always pointed in the direction of big regional theaters. I began to feel a tightness in my chest and a fluttery panic. There was a hierarchy, there was a ladder, and in order to climb it I would have to win the approval of "the boys." They would be looking over my shoulder, testing me, making sure I was "tough enough," in the way they were quite certain that directors needed to be "tough."

In my childhood growing up in the sixties, I never had the thought that being a girl could get in the way of my doing exactly whatever I wanted to do. I do believe there is a special kind of girl who has directing impulses from a very early age. We are called "bossy girls." We want to shape reality to be like we think it should be. We like to organize play; we like to make events for others to come see; we like to be in charge of telling the story. We tell the other kids we're playing with that they should be this way, not that way, that they're doing it wrong, that they should be angrier or sadder or funnier. I recognize little girls like this all the time, and I deeply love them.

My first real urges to direct a play came on a trip to Chicago in fifth grade, when my parents took me and my brother to see *You're a Good Man, Charlie Brown*. I was deeply affected by the "truth" I felt was being reflected on-stage. When I got home, I ordered a copy of the script from our local bookstore and organized some friends to be in the cast. I assigned all the parts, which included casting myself as both Lucy and Snoopy, the two best parts. Not long after, the interest of the other girls quickly dwindled; my friends stopped coming to play practice. I started to figure out then that when I was creating these events, I had to share. Girls, I think, are taught much more quickly than boys that there are limits to how bossy you get to be. And I think, in general, that this is a good thing. I think more boys need to learn this lesson about sharing; they need to learn it early and often. The world would be much better off.

And yet, like most girls entering their teens, I learned this lesson too well. My girlhood confidence and "bossiness" certainly weakened in adolescence. I absorbed the message about sharing so well that by the time I entered the first "all female" directing class at graduate school (there were two of us), I was startled to find that my male professors and all the male directors in other classes just assumed they should be in charge and make all the decisions. They had no questions about why they should be the authorities. Director was a role they assumed with confidence and ease. This made no sense to me. My female directing compatriot and I felt out of place with all the assumptions in this very male world.

I remember one of my professors, whose claim to fame was from directing a few successful Hollywood films in the fifties, telling me in confidence a story he thought would be helpful. He told of a time when he was directing Kirk Douglas in a movie. They had a disagreement, and his impulse was to want to "punch Kirk out." But then, he went on, he managed to rein in these impulses and instead put his arm around Kirk, saying in a friendly way, "Let's see if we can talk through this and find a compromise."

To me, this story epitomized the huge gulf between me and the all-male directing faculty. I have never had an impulse to want to "punch out" an actor in my entire life. My problem was quite the opposite, especially in the beginning—to find the confidence I needed to give voice to my perceptions and ideas so they could at least be on level ground with the ideas of the actors and other artists in the room. It's why I felt so strongly that I needed to make my own space so I could figure it out and find my voice organically, in my own

ALL THE LIGHTS ON

way. I thought often of the story of Georgia O'Keeffe in her early years, shutting herself away in a room and drawing a line, over and over again, for days and days, until she felt that that line was truly her own, coming from her own authentic self.

I admire women who decide to take on the hierarchy directly, fiercely proving themselves against the standards of the dominant culture, and who, once inside, set out to change the system as best they can. I just knew fairly quickly that I could never do that. I simply wouldn't survive as an artist. I knew that as I tried to withstand the pressures to conform to this male-dominated world, taking the test punches they gave out and finding ways to get back up on my feet, my authentic creativity would almost surely wither. I'd had very strong tastes of how it all worked in graduate school, with all my male professors, and I could easily tell that, with a few notable exceptions, the "are-you-man-enough test system" was even more strongly in place in the actual theater world.

MAKING MY OWN PLACE   It all made me feel tired. Not only would the structures of most theaters keep me from reaching the audiences I yearned for, but they would also prevent me from being myself as an artist. All of this punching and testing had nothing to do with anything that really mattered to me. I needed to make my own place. Without really realizing what I was doing, I set out to create a place where I would feel safe, a place where I felt unjudged and unconstrained, free to let whomever I was as an artist blossom. For me, the strongest way to face down the misogyny of the theater world was to turn around and not face it at all. By necessity, I began to make up another world for myself.

This decision meant reinventing everything from scratch. It was slow and plodding—often comical—but for me it was necessary. It's actually, for better or for worse, how I've approached most projects in my life. I have a mistrust of big systems; I need to understand *why* something is done before I commit to doing it. I wanted to carefully feel out each step of the way as I built the infrastructure for Ten Thousand Things, determining whether it was truly needed. Once again, having never really worked much in conventional theaters beyond a few assistant director jobs in Los Angeles, I started from a place of ignorance; I didn't really know how things were usually "done." I figured out how to set up my own nonprofit with software from a legal press. (I did latch on to the nonprofit model; I didn't have time to think about reinventing that wheel. Though perhaps today if I were starting up a company I'd rethink that, too, now having educated myself a bit about the roots and origins of that particular system.) I learned how to write grant proposals, puzzled out what a budget was and how to write one. The "how to create your own nonprofit" instruction book I was following at the time said I needed a board of directors of at least three people to meet at least once a year. So for a few years I had three friends over for lunch once every summer, really having no idea what we should be doing.

THE PURSUIT OF MOTHERHOOD AND ART In my early thirties, still living in Los Angeles, I also wanted to have a child. I wanted to have one as fiercely as I wanted to find work that let me give back with all my being. The problem was that the world had never presented women with any good ways to balance the desires for work and for children. I didn't have any role models. My mom and most of her friends graduating from college in the fifties generally seemed to have given up their career dreams to become mothers. Sometime after the first *Good Person* tour, I discovered I was pregnant. I found a tiny, jeweled box and inside it I put a small piece of paper on which I wrote a promise to myself not to give one up for the other. I knew ultimately the two were not in competition with each other but intertwined. I wrapped the little box in a beautiful silk cloth and kept it in my top dresser drawer, a visual reminder of that promise every time the drawer was opened. I knew, deep down, that my child would be so much better off with a mother who could live out her dreams, and I knew that as an artist, my child would inspire me. I think Shen Te's ferocious promises to her unborn child were also ringing in my mind, but unlike Shen Te, I didn't want to have to choose between two sides. I wanted a life that would let me give back through my work with kindness and generosity and intelligence and imagination—and I wanted a child.

The main challenge, I knew, would be balancing time. To allow my art and my child to nourish each other, I needed to keep time firmly under my control, making sure one set of demands didn't take much away from the other. Of course at this point, sustaining myself financially as an artist was impossible; I needed other jobs that could be done at home in my own time. I proofread and summarized depositions for law firms; I taught ESL classes at night when my baby was sleeping. I was always on the lookout for flexible work that took very little of my own energy. (My husband at the time was a freelance writer. Our marriage was ultimately unable to survive, in part because of the tensions and struggles over allocation of time and money. Ten years later we would divorce.) Throughout that first year of pregnancy and infancy, I kept trying to learn and plan for the next project, the *Electra* tour. Blurry eyed, I worked on the script, wrote grant proposals, and figured out budgets during Molly's naps.

When Molly was nine months old, she began to walk. I had taken her to visit a small cooperative day-care center in our little Venice neighborhood. Luckily, this child was also an early talker, and soon began to pound on the door, chanting one word, "School! School!"—most likely having sensed how much more fun things could be among other small people her own age. I gladly obliged. Day care, even just three or four half-days a week, suddenly allowed me room to breathe and carved out a space for me to build up my powers of concentration for my work.

By then I'd rounded up a few small grants and arranged a small tour of *Electra* to juvenile correctional facilities and youth groups. Somehow, I stumbled through rehearsals. I was working with many of the same actors who had worked on *The Good Person;* this perhaps explains their generosity toward my directing work, which at the time felt very inadequate. It was so much harder than I'd imagined to come up with the energy required to nurture a one-year-old and to direct a play at the same time. I kept eyeing that little bundle in my dresser, drawing from it, as well as from Shen Te, as much strength and determination as I could.

The tour, despite my real or imagined inadequacies, still offered exhilarating moments of connection, both with the girls in juvenile detention and with our one paying audience.

And then we felt it might be time to move. As two freelancers, my then husband and I found the prospect of raising a child in Los Angeles daunting. We needed a city where we could afford a little house and could use the public schools, as well as one full of excellent actors. I also needed a city (unlike Los Angeles) with a strong and vibrant culture of support for theater. That narrowed it down to Minneapolis. It still is shocking to me to think that our nation affords only one or two cities where such a life is possible.

Once we'd landed in our affordable little Twin Cities house, complete with a picket fence, it took another year to get the company going again. I had to find new grant sources, learn about the community, meet actors, and find new low-income performance venues. I discovered a rehearsal space in a Quaker meeting house I occasionally attended, a bare room where on Sundays people sat in a circle of folding chairs as they silently worshiped. (This circular configuration must have seeped its way into my brain to help inspire the idea of performing in the round a few years down the road. And, of course, I liked going to Meeting sometimes because of its bare-bones worship service, with nothing to look at except the other people seated around the circle engaging in their own private forms of worship. I thought it was theater of the very best kind.)

I took a short class about starting arts nonprofits. I finally learned what a board of directors could do: raise money. Out of necessity, though, I again started the board with a few good friends, none of whom were wealthy. I was temping and teaching ESL classes, too, all the while chasing after an active two-year-old. We had found a good parent co-op day care nearby where Molly spent part of the day. I really wanted to spend half of my daytime with this fun little creature, who shared with me her wonder and joy at the world, inspiring and weirdly energizing me, although I was always exhausted by day's end. I managed to get theater work done in the mornings when my brain worked best.

MAKING IT UP AS I WENT ALONG   I can now see that I found the energy and drive to keep doing all the paperwork and running around necessary to get a small

ALL THE LIGHTS ON

theater going at the same time I was raising a toddler because I was making everything up myself. In particular, this meant that I was able to choose the values I wanted to shape the organization around rather than try to fit my work into some preexisting structure. I was able to choose the values that energized and motivated me, values that were also, of course, organic to the work. As was my habit, I pared everything down to the essence. The values such work demanded seemed to all come down to two things: gifts and good pay for artists.

Whatever "plan" I had in mind for the company's finances had always been centered on gifts. The organization would receive gifts from others, which it would use to pay artists as much as possible, enabling them to give the gift of theater to those who had never had a chance to receive such a gift before. The thought of asking low-income centers to pay for a performance never once occurred to me. That would truly be robbing Peter to pay Paul. The performances would be a gift, but these new audiences in turn would give us as artists the gift of their rich life experiences and their honest responses.

So, of course, I began with the most obvious gifts, those that came from grant-making organizations: the government, private foundations, and sometimes corporations. And here I must stress that I consider it a great blessing, despite all the energy it took, that when the company started out, I was able at first to be my own "arts administrator." I learned so much. Writing grant proposals helped me to clearly articulate exactly what I was trying to do. And I think that the proposals I wrote were more vivid and interesting to read because I wrote authentically as an artist. Crafting my own budgets made me very aware of every dollar that was spent, being extremely careful at first never to spend money that I didn't know I already had in the bank. It all felt organic because I could connect the paperwork directly to the human and artistic values that motivated me.

But sometimes my plodding reinvention of everything was indeed comical. Although I had seen lists of individual donors in theater programs, of course, I hadn't really conceived of the possibility that individuals, as well as foundations, might want to give money to our work. It wasn't until I'd been in the Twin Cities for a few years that the idea occurred to me, probably as I wracked my brain for ways to come up with more money to pay people more. It was scary, but I wrote personal letters out by longhand—each several pages, to friends around the country—and was truly amazed when checks were sent back, some of them quite large (at the time, this meant over a hundred dollars). Though it was hard to ask people I knew personally for money, the thought of the brave and heartfelt efforts of the artists I worked with and their struggles to make a barely decent living fueled me. In some ways, it motivated me even more powerfully than the thought of the underserved audiences the money could help us reach, I suppose because it was even more personal—the actors were my friends. The simplicity of our production values, not needing to pay for a building, or lights, or elaborate trappings, allowed me to truly focus on artists' pay. I could become passionate about fund-raising because of this focus. In addition to wanting to make life a little easier for my friends, I did not want theater to become a profession where only those with preexisting wealth could afford to practice it.

BRINGING IN THE CRITICS   The biggest obstacles to my fund-raising, actually, were knee-jerk responses that came from many people when they first learned that we "did plays in prisons." Most people automatically assumed that our work was therefore mediocre and uninteresting, that we must just put on "bad skits." I needed a concrete way to quickly establish that our work was artistically excellent. And for this, I confess, I turned to critics. I needed their quotes so I could use them in grant proposals. It was as simple as that. I tried for several years without success to get critics to come see a show, but finally a young woman from a weekly alternative paper came to see *The Caucasian Chalk Circle* in a shelter. Amazement and surprise were expressed and praises were sung. I got another critic to come see *The Tempest* at a women's prison. More glowing reviews followed; more quotes were generated to put in the grant proposals. And slowly more regular theatergoers started to come see the shows.

Also perhaps somewhat comically, as part of my plan of "gifts from gifts," I had really never considered the possibility of earning much income from ticket sales. I had always wanted to perform once or twice for the general public just to be sure the work spoke to experienced theatergoers as well, but in my mind that really just meant a few performances for friends. Again, part of the entire genesis of the work was to avoid having to plead desperately to get reluctant audiences to buy tickets. But as word of mouth in Minneapolis grew, along with critical acclaim, I began to see that an enthusiastic paying audience could be a door to more gifts. We slowly began to add more shows where people paid for tickets to help support the free performances. And then those people, excited by the quality of the work they saw as well as our mission, became individual donors, too.

WORK AND CHILD INTERTWINED   The organization of support for the work took shape around the values of including everyone, gifts, and artist pay. I still wasn't making much money from it, but it was exactly the work I wanted to be doing, and my time was still very much under my control, allowing me to be there for my child. I could have rehearsals during the day while she was at school, and I could schedule many of our performances during the day, too, making sure to be done by the time she got off the school bus. (Hilariously, I used to start rehearsals at 9 AM because Molly was off to school by then. This went on until some desperately tired actors, with the active late-night lives of most performers, begged for us not to start until 10.) My time was my own, and that has always been worth tens of thousands of dollars to me.

Molly became old enough to come to some rehearsals, although I was careful never to use them as convenient day care. I wanted them to be a special occasion, where she could be surprised and delighted by what she saw. I have noticed that children who grow up around theater artists are often pretty great. Perhaps it's because they get to hang out with adults, especially actors, who treat children with great respect, as equals in many ways. Actors are adults who take "play" as seriously as children do; children experience enormous validation from this. These same children, I've observed, seem emotionally healthy and comfortable somehow—perhaps because they've been exposed to the wide range of human emotions as they watch rehearsals, with the distance and perspective that comes from knowing the emotions aren't "really real." They seem relaxed around emotional extremes and their rapid fluctuation; they've had practice observing them all. I remember in particular Molly walking into a rehearsal of *The Ballad of the Sad Cafe* during the scene where Miss Amelia and Marvin Macy were having a wrestling match. When Molly saw Miss Amelia punch Marvin in the face, she burst into tears and ran to hide behind a table. The actors, Carolyn Goelzer and Terry Hempleman, stopped what they were doing and very kindly and gently showed Molly just how a stage punch worked, with its sound coming from a slap of the thigh by the hand not throwing the punch. Molly relaxed, her sniffles turning into giggles, and she sat happily to watch the entire scene as we rehearsed.

Although Molly at age ten firmly declared to me that, while she enjoyed theater, it wasn't her "passion" (writing was), occasionally I would find a small part for her to play in at least some of the performances on tour (with a child-sized puppet standing in for her when she couldn't be in a particular performance). She loved being included, her imagination was stretched as she was asked to inhabit a character, and she gained confidence and pride in her own voice as an artist.

And as much richness as theater artists provided Molly's life, Molly gave back many things that were equally as important. She gave me, as a theater artist, a deep sense of connection to all the other humans before me and around me who had themselves raised children. And because I was so determined to be sure she received her fair share of my time, she brought a wonderful economy to the organization, making me focus fiercely on the mission, avoiding at all costs any unnecessary work or distractions. She kept Ten Thousand Things' focus clear and tight.

ORGANIC GROWTH   The growth of the company in the first dozen years was slow but organic. Until Molly was ten, I still did all the fund-raising and administrative work myself. Because of my focus on artist pay, I was always reluctant to spend money on any other staff. But finally, as the board of directors attracted people with more actual experience with nonprofits, they convinced

The author's daughter, Molly, at the curtain call for *Carousel*, Skyline Housing, 2003.

me to get someone to help out. In the bounteous world of Minneapolis arts philanthropy, we found a grant for hiring new part-time staff, and we found a wonderful woman (her name also Michelle) of great intelligence and kindness who was also a young mother. Like so many such remarkable women at that age, she had a desire for flexible time and the ability to work from home. Our "organizational structure" could easily accommodate that. E-mail allowed us to communicate, so no office rent was required. One more staff person made a noticeable difference in helping our income grow more quickly so we could pay artists better.

As someone else stepped in to take over more grant writing and budget tracking, I found myself with more time to dig into my artistic work—and with my child now in school full time, I do believe the plays became even richer and fuller. Several years later, it became clear that Michelle Woster, our managing director, could do better work if someone could help out with monitoring individual donations and keeping track of the box office, and so we found a grant to bring in another intelligent and kind woman to help, Amy Tang, another young mother who wanted flexible time, working from home.

WHO WILL DRIVE THE VAN?   Because of my unfamiliarity with the ways of conventional theater, I had never understood exactly what a stage manager did, especially because our work had no lighting or sound cues. At the beginning, I tried to do everything myself, including setting up the stage. At one point, however, I remember that an ironing board I'd set up for an actress to use in a scene collapsed during the show, and I acknowledged that it really was too difficult to both direct and focus properly on the mechanical details necessary to make the production run smoothly. With at least this acknowledgment of my own limitations, I then managed to pay someone a little bit to help out with gathering props and being on book during rehearsals to help the actors learn their lines. There also were some jobs around production that I just didn't want to do. When we discovered we had enough money to rent a van for the tour so that actors didn't have to haul set pieces in their cars, I knew I didn't want to have to drive the van. I drew a line. Magically, around that time another amazing young woman emerged (not a mother) who not only truly liked to do all those things but who could weld and hammer as well as sew, making repairs when needed, the marvelous Nancy Waldoch. She was wonderful at interacting with people, too, with great patience and kindness—and thus, a production manager position became apparent and sprung into place. Gradually, we passed over to her the duties of setting up and arranging the tours. I found myself with still more time to do artistic work, planning and dreaming. But because, for a while at least, I'd done most everything myself, I had a personal understanding of how most everything worked, knowledge I still greatly value.

Now, more than twenty years after we began, it feels like we're pretty much the right size, almost just big enough. We are a staff of just six, three of whom are artists (myself, Peter Vitale, our music director, and Kira Obolensky, our playwright-in-residence with full salary and benefits thanks to the Andrew W. Mellon Foundation). We still have no need of an office. We just begin every Monday by e-mailing each other our lists of what we plan to do over the course of the week and trust each other to get it done. Through such trust and friendship, we've been able to create an organization that supports the artistic work with the least amount of infrastructure necessary. It's enough. We do just three productions a year. There is no burning desire on anyone's part to do more. No one wants to do theater in the summer, the only three months of good weather in Minnesota. No one wants to work so hard that they burn out. Life is rich with things other than theater.

This sense that there is more to life than theater gives a quality to the Twin Cities acting community as well that I think is fairly unique, and for which I am most grateful: playfulness. It's almost as if because no one here seriously entertains the idea that they will someday become rich or famous through theater, let alone film or TV, that each actor is actually more focused on her or his craft, and thus able to embrace much more fully that the heart of all truly excellent acting is openness: playing, exploring, taking chances and making a fool of oneself. No one here has an agent for theatrical work; we deal with each other as human beings. And, though challenging, it is possible as an actor here to have a family and even raise children, which also helps to deflate any tendencies to self-obsession. The acting community here feels generous and supportive of each other. I consider many of its members to be my very best friends.

I am probably one of the few people from my Ivy League class who is still nowhere near making a six-figure income. But I have enough. And I am happy. My work offers its own kind of riches and rewards, not the least of which is that my time is pretty much my own with which to do whatever I want whenever I want. And I would feel profoundly uncomfortable earning, on an hourly basis at least, a whole lot more than the most experienced artists and staff of

Ten Thousand Things. I certainly would not be happy making multiple times more per hour than the people I work with. I fail to understand artistic leaders who are. At Ten Thousand Things, perhaps in part because of our connection to our audiences who have very few things, we are committed to the notion that all our boats need to rise together.

So no matter what, though we feel "big enough," Ten Thousand Things will always keep trying to raise artist pay, which will then make us feel more comfortable with raising our own pay as staff. This is one way we have come to think of "growth." And, like Johnny Appleseed, we have started to spread this unique model for doing theater that we have created by taking it to other communities and theaters that want to try it out for themselves. It's another way we've come to look at "growing."

Sometimes Ten Thousand Things feels more like an organism than an organization to me. A living and breathing being of its own right. The little seedling grew organically, supported by the strong stake of the values of inclusion, generosity, gifts, and artist pay; other shoots and tendrils naturally arose as needed to wind themselves around the stake. We created what was necessary, adapting some old structures and inventing new forms and practices to fit our very specific circumstances. We've managed to keep everything at a very human scale. There is almost no hierarchy; we communicate on a level playing field with humor and generosity. We have wine at our staff and board meetings. I still cook all the food for cast parties and donor gatherings at my home (though sometimes I do long for a caterer. But there could be worse problems). I think everyone feels respected and valued, with room to be funny and playful and honest, both at work and in their other lives.

Sometimes I hear stories of behind-the-scenes personal dramas and politics and backstabbing taking place at larger theaters. It's made me see that Ten Thousand Things' focus on connecting with our audiences from very different worlds has really helped to keep egos at bay. When we step into a room full of inmates, the anxieties and whinings of the ego seem petty and puling. I am grateful for the intensity of this focus, the clarity it gives to our priorities, and

ALL THE LIGHTS ON

the ethical behavior it encourages. This focus has helped to create a radiant organization that supports and amplifies the radiance of the actors onstage and the radiance of the audience in their honesty and surprise, which causes us to want to focus on them still more, making one big circle. It really does feel like, as much as possible, all the lights are on.

The author introduces *Man of La Mancha* at a women's correctional facility, 2011.

EPILOGUE

WHAT THIS BOOK IS FOR
Ending Words, Beginning Words

I'M WRITING THIS BOOK in the hopes that it will provoke you and perhaps inspire you. I am not trying to argue that everyone should do theater the way Ten Thousand Things does it—there is room for all kinds of theater in this world, of course. I honestly do not want this to be a "How To Do Theater This Way" manual. I am quite protective of first-time audiences. I want them to experience only the very best that theater has to offer. Ten Thousand Things' model is for professional theater artists. If this book were to cause amateur groups or high school and college theater classes to "go do a play for prisoners" because it "would be a neat experience for the performers," I would actually be mortified. Please, please do not try to foist mediocre theater upon those who are already so often condescended to. Please be deeply honest with yourself about whether you really do have the experience and skills to give first-time audiences the absolute best, matching the truth of their hard-won experiences with your own artistry. Don't do more damage by confirming their already firmly rooted bias that theater is boring and pretentious. If, as a professional artist, however, you feel confident of your skills and talents and you feel deeply moved to try to bring theater to marginalized audiences, then of course please do, with my blessings. Just be very sure.

I do hope I have provoked you to think about "audience" differently. I hope you will no longer take them for granted. I hope you will think honestly about who you would like your audience to be and how you might better reach them. Even more importantly, I hope you will think honestly and realistically about just who your audience actually *is*. Who is actually coming to your theater right now, in terms of class and race? And why is that? If you're going to do a play about an upper-middle-class white family, that's fine, but please just be honest about who actually will or won't be interested in that story. If you're doing a whole season of work about contemporary people who are financially comfortable, be aware of that and be clear about who will really be interested in the stories you're choosing to tell. And I hope you will find ways to keep your audience present, at the front and center of your attention, during your planning work and during rehearsals, and that you will pay even greater attention to them during the performances, even if they are sitting in the dark.

I want to have provoked you to think about the hugely unequal distribution of wealth in our world and, in particular, the unequal distribution of the wealth of the arts. I hope I have drawn your attention to the poverty that results. Not only the obvious material poverty of the "have-nots" but the

Women's correctional facility, *Ragtime*, 2005.

ALL THE LIGHTS ON

Housing project,
Carousel, 2003.

Karen Wiese-Thompson, Nathan Keepers, Brian Curtis James, and Kimberly Richardson, *Il Campiello*, men's correctional facility, 2005.

dimness and narrowness of the world of the "haves." The "poverty" of those who have actually become glutted with too much theater. I began Ten Thousand Things precisely because many theater audiences seemed as if they had seen too much; their responses had actually become muted and dulled. I didn't enjoy performing for those audiences. They were so used to seeing theater through a critical lens, which allowed them to make sure they were "getting what they paid for" in terms of aesthetic quality, that they had forgotten how to connect the work to their own lives. They came to the theater not out of hunger but out of obligation.

What became clear to me, as I began to take theater around to those who did not have easy access, comparing and contrasting, is that the work of the theater that only served the audiences of the "haves" had itself become impoverished. The stories it told were cushioned by the wealth of the characters. The questions the plays explored weren't that deep. The stages were groan-

ALL THE LIGHTS ON

ing under enormous and extravagant sets and elaborate special effects at the same time its artists were straining just to make a living. The artists themselves were often motivated by career concerns, wanting to impress critics and get good reviews, hoping to land the next good job. The theater experience also just wasn't as much fun, with everyone trained to be so polite and constrained. Characters onstage and audiences came from the same kinds of worlds, and their responses were usually very similar to those of their neighbors, all seated in the darkness, unable to see each other and the artists unable to see them.

What I feel so blessed to have discovered, through my particular work, groping and stumbling along the way, is that by including everyone in the audience and telling stories that engage all of us intensely, we uncover the true wealth of humanity, which is what we share in common. Wealth increases as it is spread around.

I want to provoke you to think about how the wealth of theater is distributed. I want to spark everyone who does theater to think deeply for themselves about what isn't working in our art form. Think about what you don't like about how theater is made now. Once you've located whatever that might be for you, I hope you will think with your heart and soul about how to fix it, even if it means starting over from scratch.

I do hope that somehow all this will inspire you to invent new ways and new structures that could allow the kind of theater you've been provoked to imagine to happen. I firmly believe that this is now an integral part of the work of any theater artist—not just to create the work that appears onstage but to challenge the hierarchical structures that exist and to invent new structures that will allow it to blossom and be better supported. Our work is to question every convention—and, if need be, to make it up fresh and new. There are so many wonderful theater artists in this country already engaged in this reimagining. I am just adding my voice to the many others already out there, theaters like Cornerstone and the Foundry Theater, Sojourn Theater, and, right here in Minneapolis, Mixed Blood and Pillsbury House, Bedlam, Sod House, Wonderlust, and Theater Mu, just to name a few. Even larger institutions like the Public Theater in New York City or California Shakespeare Theater or Oregon

Shakespeare Festival or the Old Globe are all trying to stretch their wings and reach out beyond their well-established confines, all trying out their own ideas, inventing, experimenting, sometimes failing, sometimes succeeding.

I can now see that for me and Ten Thousand Things, the focus has actually been on allowing the lights in all human beings to shine as brightly as possible through theater. I am excited to see what happens as you set off into the world to make or participate in theater that feels bright and alive to you.

ALL THE LIGHTS ON

APPENDIX

TEN THOUSAND THINGS PRODUCTION HISTORY

2014

DIRT STICKS BY KIRA OBOLENSKY
Directed by Michelle Hensley
With Stephen Cartmell, Sun Mee Chomet, H. Adam Harris,
    Thomasina Petrus, and Kimberly Richardson
Sets by Irve Dell
Costumes by Sonya Berlovitz and Samuel Forney
Music and Sound by Peter Vitale

THE MUSIC MAN BY MEREDITH WILLSON
Directed by Lear deBessonet
With Luverne Seifert as Harold Hill and Sarah Agnew, Aimee K. Bryant,
    Bradley Greenwald, Jim Lichtscheidl, Dennis Spears,
    Kimberly Richardson, and Ricardo Vazquez
Music Direction by Peter Vitale
Choreography by Jim Lichtscheidl
Sets by Joel Sass
Costumes by Mary Anna Culligan
Keyboards by Jake Endres

A MIDSUMMER NIGHT'S DREAM BY WILLIAM SHAKESPEARE

Directed by Michelle Hensley
With Brittany Bradford, Sun Mee Chomet, Kurt Kwan, Elise Langer,
    Gavin Lawrence, Mo Perry, Anna Sundberg, and Karen Wiese-Thompson
Sets by Stephen Mohring
Costumes by Sonya Berlovitz
Sound by Peter Vitale

A STREETCAR NAMED DESIRE BY TENNESSEE WILLIAMS

Directed by Randy Reyes with Lear deBessonet
With Elizabeth Grullon, Kurt Kwan, Kris Nelson, and Austene Van
Sets by Dean Holzman
Costumes by Mary Anna Culligan
Sound by Peter Vitale

THE SEVEN BY WILL POWER

Directed by Sarah Rasmussen
With Katie Bradley, Aimee K. Bryant, H. Adam Harris, Kinaundrae Lee,
    Brian Sostek, Ricardo Vazquez, Joetta Wright, and Bruce A. Young
Music Direction by Peter Vitale
Choreography by Kahlil Queen and Aimee K. Bryant
Sets by Stephen Mohring
Costumes by Annie Cady

MEASURE FOR MEASURE BY WILLIAM SHAKESPEARE

Directed by Michelle Hensley

With Nathan Barlow, Zach Curtis, India Gurley, Kurt Kwan, Sonja Parks,
Luverne Seifert, Suzanne Warmanen, and Karen Wiese-Thompson

Sets by Stephen Mohring

Costumes by Amelia Cheever

Sound by Peter Vitale

VASA LISA BY KIRA OBOLENSKY

Directed by Michelle Hensley

Original Music by Peter Vitale

Choreography by Jim Lichtscheidl

With Elise Langer, Jim Lichtscheidl, Tracey Maloney, Luverne Seifert,
and Sally Wingert

Sets by Irve Dell

Costumes by Sonya Berlovitz

Additional instruments by Heather Barringer and Annie Enneking

AS YOU LIKE IT BY WILLIAM SHAKESPEARE

Directed by Lear deBessonet

With Aimee K. Bryant, Pearce Bunting, Maggie Chestovich,
Bradley Greenwald, Randy Reyes, and Kimberly Richardson

Sets by Stephen Mohring

Costumes by Mary Anna Culligan

Sound by Peter Vitale

IL CAMPIELLO BY CARLO GOLDONI, ADAPTATION BY STEVEN EPP

Directed by Michelle Hensley

With Sarah Agnew, Christiana Clark, Brian Curtis James, Nathan Keepers,
    Elise Langer, Thomasina Petrus, Randy Reyes, Kimberly Richardson,
    and Karen Wiese-Thompson

Sets by Stephen Mohring

Costumes by Amelia Cheever

Sound by Peter Vitale

MAN OF LA MANCHA BY DALE WASSERMAN, JOE DARION, MITCH LEIGH

Directed by Michelle Hensley

Musical Direction by Peter Vitale

With Steven Epp, Matt Guidry, Tracey Maloney, T. Mychael Rambo,
    Luverne Siefert, and Regina Marie Williams

Sets by Stephen Mohring

Costumes by Kelsey Glasener

Keyboards by Michael Pearce Donley

DOUBT: A PARABLE BY JOHN PATRICK SHANLEY

Directed by Peter Rothstein

With Jane Froiland, Kris Nelson, Regina Marie Williams, and Sally Wingert

Sets by Dean Holzman

Costumes by Amelia Cheever

Music by Peter Vitale

LIFE'S A DREAM BY PEDRO CALDERÓN DE LA BARCA

Directed by Michelle Hensley

With Maggie Chestovich, Stephen D'Ambrose, Celeste Jones, Elise Langer,
    Kiseung Rhee, Namir Smallwood, and Dennis Spears

Costumes by Kelsey Glasener

Props by Erica Zaffarano

Sound by Peter Vitale

MY FAIR LADY BY ALAN JAY LERNER AND FREDERICK LOEWE

Directed by Lear deBessonet

Music Direction by Peter Vitale

With Kate Eifrig, Bradley Greenwald, Steve Hendrickson,
    Kimberly Richardson, and Luverne Seifert

Choreography by Jim Lichtscheidl

Sets by Jeremy Wilhelm

Costumes by Kathy Kohl

STONES IN HIS POCKETS BY MARIE JONES

Directed by Michelle Hensley

With Steven Epp and Jim Lichtscheidl

Costumes by Kelsey Glasener

Sound by Eric Jensen

OTHELLO BY WILLIAM SHAKESPEARE

Directed by Sonja Parks and Michelle Hensley
With Ansa Akyea, Christiana Clark, Peter Hansen, Tracey Maloney,
    Kimberly Richardson, Matt Sciple, and Luverne Seifert
Set by Stephen Mohring
Costumes by Mary Anna Culligan
Sound by Peter Vitale

RASKOL BY KIRA OBOLENSKY

Directed by Michelle Hensley
Original Music by Peter Vitale
With Lisa Clair, Craig Johnson, Tracey Maloney, Kris Nelson,
    Charles Schuminski, Luverne Seifert, and Karen Wiese-Thompson
Set by Irve Dell
Costumes by Kelsey Glasener
Additional instruments by Nathan Hanson and Chris Bates

ENDGAME BY SAMUEL BECKETT

Directed by Marion McClinton
Music by Heather Barringer
With Terry Bellamy, Barbara Berlovitz, Christiana Clark,
    and Steve Hendrickson
Set by Stephen Mohring
Costumes by Vera Mariner
Sound by Heather Barringer

TWELFTH NIGHT BY WILLIAM SHAKESPEARE (ALL FEMALE)

Directed by Michelle Hensley

With Maggie Chestovich, Kate Eifrig, Barbara Kingsley,
Isabell Monk O'Connor, Sonja Parks, Kimberly Richardson,
and Sally Wingert

Set by Erica Zaffarano

Costumes by Sonya Berlovitz

Music and Sound by Peter Vitale

ONCE ON THIS ISLAND BY LYNN AHRENS AND STEPHEN FLAHERTY

Directed by Peter Rothstein

Musical direction by Peter Vitale

Choreography by Aimee K. Bryant

With Eric Avery, Michelle Carter, Celeste Jones, Kinaundrae Lee,
Kahlil Queen, Greta Oglesby, Dennis Spears, and Regina Marie Williams

Set by Erica Zaffarano

Costumes by Willene Mangham

Keyboards by Michael Donley

EURYDICE BY SARAH RUHL

Directed by Larissa Kokernot

With Lisa Clair, Marc Halsey, Steve Hendrickson, Leif Jurgenson,
Vera Mariner, and Sonja Parks

Set by Joe Stanley

Costumes by Sonya Berlovitz

Sound by Peter Vitale

RICHARD III BY WILLIAM SHAKESPEARE (ALL MALE)

Directed by Michelle Hensley
With Bob Davis, Shawn Hamilton, Craig Johnson, Darien Johnson,
    Jim Lichtscheidl, Richard Ooms, and Luverne Seifert
Sets by Stephen Mohring
Costumes by Kathy Kohl
Sound by Heather Barringer

LITTLE SHOP OF HORRORS BY HOWARD ASHMAN

Music by Alan Menken
Directed by Michelle Hensley
Music Direction by Peter Vitale
Choreography by Jim Lichtscheidl
With Kate Eifrig, Jim Lichtscheidl, Sonja Parks, Thomasina Petrus,
    Luverne Seifert, Harry Waters Jr., and Karen Wiese-Thompson
Sets by Stephen Mohring
Costumes by Vera Mariner

BLOOD WEDDING BY FEDERICO LORCA

Directed by Juliette Carrillo
With Barbara Berlovitz, Sha Cage, Maggie Chestovich, Kurt Kwan,
    and Danny Salmen
Puppets and Set by Allison Heimstead
Costumes by Emily Pepper
Music by Peter Vitale

THE MERCHANT OF VENICE BY WILLIAM SHAKESPEARE
Directed by Michelle Hensley
With Lisa Clair, Matt Guidry, Steve Hendrickson, Catherine Johnson,
    Darien Johnson, Kiseung Rhee, Stacia Rice, and David Wiles
Sets by Stephen Mohring
Costumes by Kathy Kohl
Sound by Peter Vitale

RED NOSES BY PETER BARNES
Directed by Larissa Kokernot
Music by Peter Vitale
With Lisa Clair, Kate Eifrig, Dylan Fresco, Alayne Hopkins, Kris L. Nelson,
    and Lee Mark Nelson
Set by Stephen Mohring
Costumes by Kathy Kohl

IN A GARDEN BY GERTRUDE STEIN AND KEVIN KLING
Directed by Michelle Hensley
With Jim Lichtscheidl, Tracey Maloney, and Luverne Seifert
Music by Meyer Kupferman and Peter Vitale
Sets by Michael Sommers
Costumes by Vera Mariner

2005

ANTIGONE BY SOPHOCLES, ADAPTATION BY EMILY MANN

Directed by Michelle Hensley
With Bob Davis, Kate Eifrig, Darien Johnson, Ron Menzel, Carla Noack,
 Sonja Parks, Luverne Seifert, and Patti Shaw
Set by Stephen Mohring
Costumes by Vera Mariner
Sound by Heather Barringer

RAGTIME BY TERENCE McNALLY

Directed by Michelle Hensley
Musical Direction by Marya Hart
Choreography by Jim Lichtscheidl
With Aimee K. Bryant, Bob Davis, Shawn Hamilton, Darien Johnson,
 Jim Lichtscheidl, Vera Mariner, Matt Sciple, and Sally Wingert
Sets by Julian McFaul
Costumes by Ellen Hutchinson

IPHIGENIA BY EURIPIDES

Directed by Theodora Skipitares
With Carena Crowell, Carolyn Goelzer, Casey Grieg, Kris Nelson,
 and Luverne Seifert
Puppets by Theodora Skipitares and Cecilia Schiller
Costumes by Kathy Kohl
Music by Mike Croswell

AT YOUR SERVICE! BY KEVIN KLING

Directed by Michelle Hensley
With Bradley Greenwald, Jim Lichtscheidl, and Luverne Seifert
Sets by Stephen Mohring
Costumes by Ellen Hutchinson
Sound by Heather Barringer

CYRANO DE BERGERAC BY EDMOND ROSTAND

Directed by Michelle Hensley
With Steve Hendrickson, Terry Hempleman, Darien Johnson, Ron Menzel,
    Sonja Parks, Matt Sciple, and Maren Ward
Sets by Stephen Mohring
Costumes by Ellen Hutchinson
Sound by Peter Vitale

THE WINTER'S TALE BY WILLIAM SHAKESPEARE

Directed by Tracy Young
With Aimee K. Bryant, Nathan Christopher, Kate Eifrig, Matt Guidry,
    Steve Hendrickson, and Marie-Francoise Theodore
Sets by Stephen Mohring
Costumes by Sonya Berlovitz
Sound by Peter Vitale

THE GOOD PERSON OF SZECHWAN BY BERTROLT BRECHT

Directed by Michelle Hensley

With Nathan Christopher, Stephen D'Ambrose, Kate Eifrig, Matt Guidry,
    Barbara Kingsley, Sonja Parks, Harry Waters Jr.,
    and Karen Wiese-Thompson

Sets by Stephen Mohring

Costumes by Vera Mariner

Music by Peter Vitale

CAROUSEL BY RODGERS AND HAMMERSTEIN

Directed by Michelle Hensley

Musical Direction by Peter Vitale

With Sarah Agnew, Maggie Chestovich, Carolyn Goelzer, Matt Guidry,
    Terry Hempleman, Tyrone Lewis, Jason Little, Ruth MacKenzie,
    Vera Mariner, and Matt Sciple

Sets by Joel Sass

Costumes by Amelia Cheever

Movement by Matt Guidry

Fiddle by Molly Sue McDonald

THE ISLAND BY ATHOL FUGARD

Directed by Carol MacVey

With James Austin Williams and James Young

Set by Stephen Mohring

Costumes by Kathleen Richert

KING LEAR BY WILLIAM SHAKESPEARE

Directed by Michelle Hensley

With Stephen D'Ambrose, Sam Chase, Barbara Kingsley, Jim Lichtscheidl,
Greta Oglesby, Kim Schultz, Charles Schuminski, Matt Sciple,
Luverne Seifert, Sandra Struthers, and Marie-Francoise Theodore

Sets by Stephen Mohring

Costumes by Kathleen Richert

Music by Heather Barringer

ANNA BELLA EEMA BY LISA D'AMOUR

Music by Chris Sidorsky

Directed by Michelle Hensley

Musical Direction by Peter Vitale

With Larissa Kokernot, Ruth MacKenzie, and Vera Mariner

Sets by Stephen Mohring

Costumes by Signe Albertson

MISS JULIE BY AUGUST STRINDBERG

Directed by Peter Rothstein

With Norah Long, Terry Hempleman, and Carla Noack

Sets by Stephen Mohring

Costumes by Kathleen Richert

Music by George Mauer

THE FURIES BY AESCHYLUS, WITH TEXT BY LISA D'AMOUR

Directed by Michelle Hensley
With Jennifer Blagen, Carolyn Goelzer, Jodi Kellogg, Barbara Kingsley,
    Ron Menzel, Greta Oglesby, Matt Sciple, Luverne Seifert,
    and Marie-Francoise Theodore
Set and Costumes by Sandy Spieler
Music by Becky Dale
Percussion by Heather Barringer

THE MOST HAPPY FELLA BY FRANK LOESSER

Directed by Michelle Hensley
Music Direction by Peter Vitale
With Signe Albertson, Aimee K. Bryant, Stephen D'Ambrose,
    Terry Hempleman, Vera Mariner, Matt Sciple, Marquetta Senters,
    and Esera Tuaolo
Sets by Stephen Mohring
Costumes by Kathleen Richert

WAITING FOR GODOT BY SAMUEL BECKETT

Directed by Matt Sciple
With Adena Brumer, Zach Curtis, Jim Lichtscheidl, Dale Pfeilsticker,
    and Karen Wiese-Thompson
Set by Mark Abel Garcia and Matt Sciple
Costumes by Ellen Hutchinson
Sound by Dale Pfeilsticker

ALL THE LIGHTS ON

CYMBELINE BY WILLIAM SHAKESPEARE

Directed by Michelle Hensley

With Aimee K. Bryant, Warren Bowles, Zach Curtis, Steve Hendrickson,
    Kelly Hilliard, Barbara Kingsley, Norah Long, and Charles Schuminski

Set by Stephen Mohring

Costumes by Ellen Hutchinson

Music by Mike Croswell

THE THREE LIVES OF LUCIE CABROL BY JOHN BERGER

Directed by Michelle Hensley

With Brian Baumgartner, Pete Colburn, Matt Guidry, Terry Hempleman,
    Jodi Kellogg, Larissa Kokernot, and Matt Sciple

Set by Stephen Mohring

Costumes by Ellen Hutchinson

Music by Peter Vitale

Fiddle by Molly Sue McDonald

THE TEMPEST BY WILLIAM SHAKESPEARE

Directed by Michelle Hensley

With Signe Albertson, Aimee K. Bryant, Zach Curtis, Stephen D'Ambrose,
    Steve Hendrickson, Jodi Kellogg, Barbara Kingsley, and Ron Menzel

Set by Stephen Mohring

Costumes by Ellen Hutchinson

Music by Mike Croswell

THE UNSINKABLE MOLLY BROWN BY MEREDITH WILLSON

Directed by Michelle Hensley

Music Direction by Peter Vitale

With Jodi Kellogg, Larissa Kokernot, Ron Menzel, Dale Pfeilsticker,
    Grant Richey, Carolyn Pool, Matt Sciple, and Ruth Williams

Set by Stephen Mohring

Costumes by Signe Albertson and Ellen Hutchinson

Fiddle by Char Bostrom

ALL THE LIGHTS ON

MEASURE FOR MEASURE BY WILLIAM SHAKESPEARE

Directed by Michelle Hensley

With Signe Albertson, Zach Curtis, Mary Alette Davis, Steve Hendrickson,
Barbara Kingsley, Matt Sciple, Elizabeth Teefy, Peter Vitale,
and Molly Rose Hensley-Clancy

Sets by Stephen Mohring

Costumes by Ellen Hutchinson

Music by Peter Vitale

THE BALLAD OF THE SAD CAFE BY EDWARD ALBEE AND CARSON McCULLERS AND *DROWNING* BY MARÍA IRENE FORNÉS

Directed by Michelle Hensley

With Brian Baumgartner, Carolyn Goelzer, Terry Hempleman,
Jon Micheels Leiseth, Carolyn Pool, and Matt Sciple

Set and Masks by Stephen Mohring

Costumes by Ellen Hutchinson

Music by Eric Mohring and Brian Barnes

THE EMPEROR OF THE MOON BY APHRA BEHN

Directed by Michelle Hensley

With Signe Albertson, Greg Arata, Aimee K. Bryant, Barbara Kingsley, Larissa
Kokernot, Dale Pfeilsticker, Matt Sciple, and Molly Hensley-Clancy

Set by Joe Stanley

Costumes by Ellen Hutchinson

Music by Peter Vitale

DAYS ARE SILVER NIGHTS ARE GOLD BY ERIK EHN

Directed by Michelle Hensley

With Signe Albertson, Aimee K. Bryant, Christopher Edwards,
and Molly Hensley-Clancy

Set and Costumes by Julie Archer

Music by John Banks

ALL THE LIGHTS ON

THE CAUCASIAN CHALK CIRCLE BY BERTOLT BRECHT

Directed by Michelle Hensley

With Signe Albertson, Barbara Kingsley, Larissa Kokernot, Ruth McKenzie,
Alexander Parker, Dale Pfeilsticker, Carolyn Pool, Matt Sciple,
Peter Vitale, and Molly Hensley-Clancy

Set and Costumes by Ellen Hutchinson

Music by Scott Spencer

MUD BY MARÍA IRENE FORNÉS

Directed by Michelle Hensley

With Mike McGowan, Maren Perry, and Luverne Seifert

Sets and Costumes by Ellen Hutchinson

Music by Lisa Fuglie

1995

THE KING STAG (THE QUEEN STAG) BY CARLO GOZZI

Directed by Michelle Hensley

With George Keller, Larissa Kokernot, Rhonda Lund, Mike McGowan,
    Maren Perry, and Luu Pham

Sets and Costumes by Ellen Hutchinson

1994

LIFE'S A DREAM BY PEDRO CALDERÓN DE LA BARCA

Directed by Michelle Hensley

With Brian Chapman-Evans, Don Cosgrove, Dana Farner, Mike McGowan,
    Maren Perry, William Bird Wilkens, and Ahanti Young

Sets and Costumes by Ellen Hutchinson

Music by Bob Hughes

1992

ELECTRA BY SOPHOCLES

Directed by Michelle Hensley

With Gayle Harbor, Kenneth Ransom, Lucy Rodriguez, Ivonne Coll,
    Bill Burns, and Christianne Mays

Sets and Costumes by Elizabeth Luce

Music by Gary Johnson

1991

THE GOOD PERSON OF SZECHWAN BY BERTOLT BRECHT

Directed by Michelle Hensley

With Bill Burns, Kate Cherry, Craig Fernandez, Marilyn Henkus,
    Suzanne Kato, Christianne Mays, and Kenneth Ransom

Sets and Costumes by Norma Bowles

Music by Marilyn Henkus

ALL THE LIGHTS ON